Walks in Old London

Walks in Old London

Peter Jackson

C&B

COLLINS & BROWN

FRONT AND BACK COVER *A Lithograph of Trafalgar Square in 1841 by Thomas Shotter Boyce.*

First published in Great Britain in 1993
by Collins & Brown Limited
Mercury House
195 Knightsbridge
London SW7 1RE

1 3 5 7 9 8 6 4 2

British Library Cataloguing-in-Publication Data:
A catalogue record for this book is available from the British Library.

ISBN 1 85585 158 X (hardback edition)
ISBN 1 85585 179 2 (paperback edition)

Filmset by Goodfellow & Egan, Cambridge

Reproduction by Daylight, Singapore

Printed and bound in Great Britain by Butler & Tanner, Frome, Somerset

Contents

INTRODUCTION

WE ARE TOLD THAT London is for forever changing. The greatest change of all was, of course, as a result of the Great Fire. But the rebuilt City, which retained the plan of its ancient streets and lanes, then altered very little until well into the nineteenth century. Outside its boundaries the changes were those of growth and development as London expanded into the West End and north of Oxford Street.

Real change, in the sense of demolition and rebuilding, began in the 1820s when Nash cut his triumphal route from Carlton House to Marylebone Park and formed Regent Street and Piccadilly Circus. A few years later the slum clutter of Charing Cross was swept away to emerge as Trafalgar Square, while in the City radical changes started when the rebuilding of London Bridge necessitated the formation of King William Street.

But this was just the beginning. There followed, half-way through the nineteenth century, a programme of improvement schemes for the creation of new thoroughfares, mostly designed to relieve the ever increasing pressure of traffic, which was to transform the old layout of narrow streets and alleys into the London we know today. Most of these Victorian improvements, which we now take for granted, were carried out by the Metropolitan Board of Works which, between its establishment in 1855 and its disbandment in 1889, constructed over fifteen miles of new streets. Major thoroughfares like Queen Victoria Street and Holborn Viaduct in the 1860s, and Charing Cross Road and Shaftesbury Avenue in the 1870s, meant wholesale destruction of innumerable alleys, lanes and courts with their picturesque old houses, shops and inns. In the City even some Wren churches had to go.

And with the new streets came new buildings on a scale and in a style never seen before. Huge office blocks, banks, enormous hotels and commercial buildings of every kind and in every type of architecture lined the new thoroughfares. It is this Victorian London, so destructive in the making, that is now in its turn being busily destroyed.

Futile as it is to regret the loss of the ancient and picturesque during the years of Victorian improvements, what we do have every reason to be sad about is that there are so few visual records. In the early nineteenth century a few antiquarians did their best to make some sort of record of old buildings before they were swept away, or even while they were actually being demolished. But their activities were limited. We search in vain for any drawings of the hundreds of houses which Nash destroyed, yet ironically we know exactly what every inch of his Regent Street looked like, although not a single one of his buildings exists today, with the exception of All Souls, Langham Place. This is due to the drawings of Thomas Hosmer Shepherd which were published as engravings in *Metropolitan Improvements* in 1830.

Each decade produced artists whose published drawings depicted the London of their time. Thomas Malton's aquatints in the 1790s, the street elevations produced by John Tallis in the 1830s, Shotter Boys' lithographs in the 1840s, all show us a pre-photographic London. Accurate as these drawings are, we are conscious that they are only artists' interpretations and, if the buildings no longer exist, we cannot be absolutely certain what they really looked like. But with the coming of photography we enter a new world. Now all is real; we see everything as it actually was, frozen in a moment of time.

Photography was invented two years after Queen Victoria came to the throne but the early photographs record a Georgian London; by the time the new process was perfected, it was truly depicting the Victorian London with which we are familiar.

Now London is changing again, changing as I write. It is almost impossible to look at any view of central London that is not blighted by scaffolding and cranes pulling down the old, putting up the new. It is by no means certain that the identifiable buildings in some of these old photographs will still be standing when this book appears. When I began, parts of old Blackfriars Station could still be seen. Now it is completely obliterated by a new block.

I have avoided the temptation, often with difficulty, to condemn the destruction of the old in favour of the new. This book is not a critical architectural assessment. It is a guide with which one can walk, actually or in the imagination from an armchair, through the London of the present and discover the London of the past.

The aim has been to include only pictures, whether old prints or photographs, which show some feature or building which still exists today so that, no matter how the view has changed, there is always something by which it can be identified. This has not always been possible. For instance, in the 1881 photograph showing the junction of Cannon Street and King William Street (p. 136) nothing exists today, but it retains its old shape so well that it can still be recognized.

The maps were specially drawn to show the exact viewpoint of each artist or photographer. All the maps show the streets as they are today; where the layout has drastically changed, another map has been added showing its original appearance.

ACKNOWLEDGEMENTS

It is impossible to record all the volumes consulted in the writing of this book but a few must be mentioned as being of particular value.

Two underrated books, *London Rebuilt* and *London Marches On*, both by Harold Clunn, who delighted in recording even the most minor changes; *History of Street Improvements 1855–1897* by Percy J. Edwards, dull reading but statistically invaluable; the London volumes in the *Buildings of England* series edited by Nikolaus Pevsner, vital for dates and descriptions of individual buildings; Gavin Stamp's wonderful *The Changing Metropolis*, which gives an incomparable view of London in photographs up to 1879; and, of course, happy is the researcher who finds his area covered by one of the volumes in the great *Survey of London*, which will have done all the hard work for him.

I must acknowledge my great debt of gratitude to Ian Leith of the National Monuments Record, who helped me so much with advice and suggestions.

KNIGHTSBRIDGE TO COVENT GARDEN

ABOVE *Piccadilly Circus from Piccadilly.*

THIS WALK STARTS at one of the world's most famous department stores, standing in what was once open countryside and market gardens, a rural approach to Hyde Park Corner, where London itself began. Indeed the first house you come to, Apsley House, still retains the nickname, 'Number One London'. It was a grand entrance.

In a very real sense it was also the entrance to Buckingham Palace, which set the tone for the whole area. In the eighteenth century Mayfair was created to the north of Piccadilly and great houses were built facing the open fields, later to become Green Park. The few remaining Victorian and Edwardian mansions which later replaced them appear to be residential but most are now offices. Half-way along that part of Piccadilly which faces Green Park, the character of the buildings suddenly changes and becomes aggressively twentieth-century; nothing here sur-vives earlier than 1920. Even the mighty Ritz Hotel, which looks as if it has been there forever, dates only from 1906 and, with its pavement colonnade, brings a touch of Paris into the heart of London.

Piccadilly now becomes the great shopping street of the West End with the world's most famous grocers, Fortnum & Mason's, and London's oldest book-shop, Hatchards.

On to Piccadilly Circus, the Times Square of London and still the focal point of the West End, though a circus no longer since they shifted Eros for the umpteenth time. The blare of entertainment which characterizes the Circus today is echoed as we go along what is now London's most tawdry thoroughfare, Coventry Street, into Leicester Square. This has been a centre of rowdy entertainment since the earliest times and the tradition continues, as it does at Covent Garden where the walk ends. For this was the popular resort of the man-about-town throughout the eighteenth century and now that the fruit and vegetable market has gone it is once again a centre for wining and dining, with the Royal Opera House and Drury Lane Theatre thrown in.

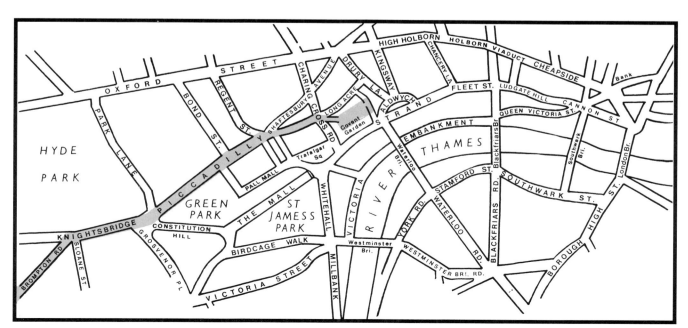

A   C1905

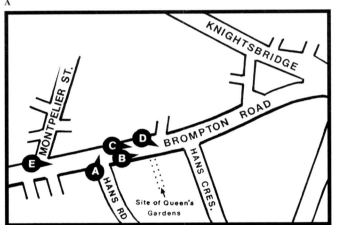

Brompton Road

Brompton Road has undergone many changes over the years. The quiet country road began to be built upon in the eighteenth century, with modest houses with front gardens, and some of these houses are to be seen in these Edwardian photographs.

It was as a direct route to the International Exhibition of 1862 (built on a site now occupied by the Natural History Museum) that sleepy Brompton Road came into prominence. The creation of 'Museum Land' at South Kensington further increased its importance as the main road to London's new cultural centre; the thoroughfare was widened and the houses' front gardens removed.

The changes on the north side have been traumatic and all the buildings opposite Harrods seen here **(A and B)** have been replaced by modern blocks, some as recently as the 1980s.

B   C1905

C
C1900

D
C1904

A *The north side of Brompton Road, some of the houses surviving from the eighteenth century. They have all now been demolished.*

B *Farther along the north side, directly opposite Harrods, whose* art nouveau *windows are clearly seen on the right.*

C *South side of Brompton Road showing, on the right, the Buttercup pub on the corner of Queen's Gardens, both of which were swallowed up by the expansion of Harrods westwards.*

D *The present frontage of Harrods being built in 1903.*

E *Everything in this 1908 photo of Harrods still exists today; only the traffic has changed. The building on the left dates from 1850 and the one on the right was designed by the architect of Harrods, C.W. Stephens.*

Harrods

IT WAS IN 1853 that Charles Henry Harrod, formerly a wholesale tea-merchant from the City, opened a small grocer's shop in the middle of the terrace in photograph **(C)**. The business flourished and the 1870s saw an extension added to the back and premises acquired on either side. At the same time new departments were added selling perfumery, medicine and stationery together with flowers and fruit.

A fire in 1883 provided the opportunity for further expansion and **(C)**, which was taken about 1900, shows its appearance when re-built. New property was acquired and leases bought, so that by 1894 it was decided to redevelop the whole site from Hans Crescent to Hans Road and erect a store 'of very substantial character'. It was designed by C.W. Stephens and building began in 1901. The Hans Crescent corner was erected first, followed by the two storeys of shops temporarily roofed over and opened for business, leaving the superstructure to be added later **(D)**. The frontage we see now **(E)** was completed in 1905.

E
1908

A   1896

B   1883

A *Knightsbridge looking east in 1896.*

B *Photograph taken in 1883. The advertising hoardings mark the site where Hyde Park Court was to be built.*

C *Further along Knightsbridge with Albert Gate on the left and William Street on the right.*

D *Nearing Hyde Park Corner, two cabbies chat together as they are about to pass Holy Trinity Chapel.*

Knightsbridge

AT THE JUNCTION of Knightsbridge and Brompton Road (A), the huge block of residential apartments called Hyde Park Court, built in 1889, dominates the scene. In 1904 the interior was damaged by fire and the building was reopened as a hotel four years later. It catered to the very cream of society and was frequently patronized by members of the royal family who had their own private entrance in the park for their use only. Today the Hyde Park Hotel, virtually unaltered, remains one of the grandest and most exclusive of the Edwardian hotels still flourishing in London.

Hyde Park Court dwarfs the row of substantial Georgian houses by its side. These incongruous reminders of the days when Knightsbridge was a country suburb were sold in 1935 for £500,000 but remained derelict until 1942 when they were finally cleared away. Bowater House now occupies the site.

The statue in the middle of the road was erected in 1895 only a year before the photograph was taken. It is of Lord Strathnairn, a now-forgotten Victorian soldier, who spent sixty-five years in the Army, fought in the Crimea, and ended up a Field Marshal. But Victorian soldiers must give way to the advance of traffic and he retreated in 1933.

The small buildings on the right which stand on the corner of Sloane Street were completely rebuilt when the Underground arrived in 1906, but on the other corner Harvey Nichols has hardly changed since it was built in 1892.

Almost all that remains to be seen today are the twin buildings on either side of Albert Gate (C). These were built by Thomas Cubitt in 1844 and were thought at the time to be so enormous that they were nicknamed Malta and Gibraltar 'because they would never be taken'. In fact, within a year of its being

C

C1886

built the eastern one, seen clearly in the photograph, was taken by Henry Hudson ('The Railway King') who purchased it for £15,000 at the height of that railway mania in which he figured so prominently. When his financial empire crashed, the house was bought by the French government for use as its embassy and has been the French Embassy ever since.

Next door can be seen the shop of James Shout, Dealer in Choice Jewels & Antique Plate. He had started out in business on the other side of Knightsbridge so when he opened his shop here he put a notice in his window, 'Shout from opposite'. But in 1899 this shop was pulled down to make an extension to the French Embassy and he went across the road yet again where he displayed a new sign, 'Shout back from opposite'.

On the left stands Holy Trinity Chapel (D) known locally as 'Heaven between two Hells' because it was flanked by a pub on either side. It stood until 1905 when most of these buildings on the north side were demolished to make way for the huge block of flats called Parkside.

D

C1890

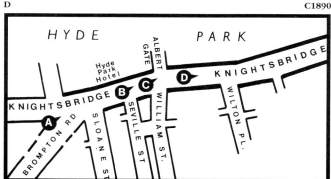

13

A   1797

Hyde Park Corner 1

IT IS EASY TO SEE why Apsley House, the first house on the left as the traveller passed through the Turnpike on entering the metropolis, came to be nicknamed 'No. 1 London'. The original redbrick house was built for Baron Apsley in 1778 and became the home of the Duke of Wellington in 1817. In 1829 it was refaced in stone and given the Corinthian portico we see today.

The toll-gates were removed in 1825 and at the same time Decimus Burton's beautiful Ionic screen at the entrance to Hyde Park was erected.

The shadow of the Duke of Wellington on horseback, seen in the lithograph on the right, is being cast by his equestrian statue standing on the Wellington Arch, which appears in the view below.

A *The turnpike gate with St George's Hospital on the right in 1797.*

B *Apsley House in 1810.*

C *The view in 1842.*

D *The shadow of the Duke of Wellington falls on Apsley House.*

E *So many members of the Rothschild family occupied the great mansions to be seen just beyond Apsley House that this was called Rothschild Row. The new Park Lane traffic exit swept them away in 1960.*

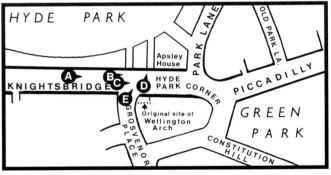

B   1810

C   1842

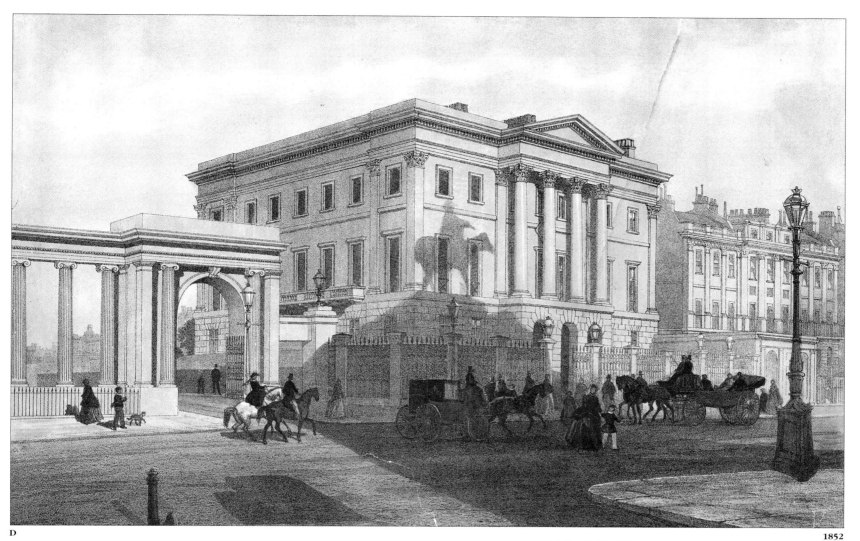

D   1852

E   C1890

A

A *Hyde Park Corner in 1828 showing the arch at the top of Constitution Hill in its original position parallel with the Hyde Park screen.*

B *The arch surmounted by the equestrian statue of the Duke of Wellington erected in 1846.*

C *Arch and screen still parallel in 1876 show the grand architectural scheme as originally intended.*

D *Wellington's statue was removed and the arch re-sited to its present position in 1883. On the left is Boehm's statue of the Duke put up in 1888.*

E *In 1912 the quadriga gave the arch its present appearance though it is now isolated from traffic.*

B

C1875

1828

WELLINGTON ARCH, GREEN PARK.

D C1890

C 1876

E C1914

Hyde Park Corner 2

WHERE SHEEP COULD safely graze in 1828 is now the busiest traffic junction in London. The maps on the right show the changes which have taken place over the years. Only the Ionic screen, designed by Decimus Burton in 1825, remains unmoved and unaltered. It was conceived originally, not as the entrance to Hyde Park, but as the grand entrance, through its companion arch across the road, and down Constitution Hill, to Buckingham Palace.

The arch, also by Decimus Burton, was never completed as he intended it. His original design included statues and a frieze with the arch surmounted by a quadriga, a triumphal chariot drawn by four horses. This was not forthcoming, but in 1846 Matthew Wyatt's huge statue of the Duke of Wellington on his horse Copenhagen, 30 feet (9 metres) high and weighing 40 tons, was erected on top of the arch. Burton condemned it; the public ridiculed it; even Queen Victoria disliked it but, not wanting to offend the Duke, she withdrew her request for its removal and it was allowed to remain.

In 1883 the redesign of Hyde Park Corner necessitated the demolition of Burton's arch and the Duke's Statue was removed to Aldershot where it stands today. The arch, rebuilt on a different axis further down Constitution Hill, remained unadorned until 1912 when it at last received its quadriga, 'Peace Descending into the Chariot of War' by Adrian Jones.

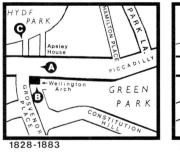

1828-1883

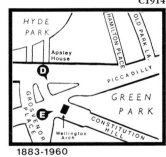

1883-1960

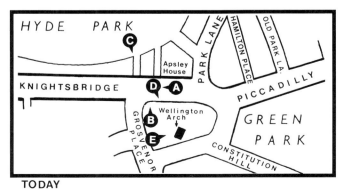

TODAY

A   C1896

Published Dec 1 1807 by 1st Malcolm The late Lord Barrymores house Piccadilly

B   1807

Piccadilly

In the 1760s the western half of Piccadilly began to be built upon, for the northern side, with its uninterrupted view over Green Park, was an ideal site for building a town house with a rustic prospect. Two such houses are depicted in the 1807 etching on the left, one of which can be seen over the omnibus in the photograph above and which has miraculously survived today. Built about 1761, it was a private house until 1847 when it became a raffish gambling den called the Coventry Club. In 1868 it was taken over by the St James's Club but in 1975 financial difficulties forced them to leave and merge with Brooks's.

The second house in the print was once the Pultney Hotel where the Emperor of Russia stayed in 1814 with his sister. She was very complimentary about the hotel's water-closets which had the advantage of discharging directly into the Tyburn River which flowed through the gap clearly seen in the print. The house was partly demolished and rebuilt in 1851 with a frontage deceptively similar to the original.

The Georgian houses above were replaced by the Park Lane Hotel in 1927 but in the other Victorian photograph all the foreground buildings remain today, unaltered. The rest of Piccadilly, from Half Moon Street up to the Ritz, was completely rebuilt in the 1920s.

A *The Park Lane Hotel replaced this row of Georgian houses in 1927.*

B *This etching, dated 1807, shows the present Nos. 105 and 106 with the gap where the Tyburn River flowed.*

C

1895

C These Victorian and Edwardian mansions, once private houses, still exist. The gate on the right leads to Palmerston House where the great statesman lived for ten years until his death in 1865. It became the Naval and Military Club nicknamed the 'In and Out' because of the signs on the gates.

D Behind the wall stood Devonshire House, demolished in 1924, and across the road Walsingham House was built in 1887 as a block of residential flats.

E Walsingham House was demolished in 1904 and construction started on the Ritz Hotel which was completed in 1906. Designed by the same architects who had built the Paris Ritz, it was very French in style with a Louis XVI interior and a pavement colonnade reminiscent of the Rue de Rivoli.

D   C1904

E   C1908

19

A

B   C1895

D   1834

Piccadilly – North Side

BY 1839 WHEN JOHN TALLIS was publishing his street elevations, Piccadilly, originally lined with noblemen's mansions, had become a street of small plain-fronted buildings with ground floor shops displaying all manner of goods behind their multi-paned windows (**A**).

By the 1890s most of these buildings had gone, having been replaced by much larger, flamboyant blocks, one of which still stands on the corner of Old Bond Street (**B**).

Burlington House (**C**) is the only great mansion still surviving. The front we see today dates only from 1873. Before that the mansion was protected from public gaze by a plain brick wall (**E**) also seen in Tallis's elevation. Next to it Tallis shows the original entrance to Burlington Arcade (**D**). This was built in 1819 to prevent people throwing rubbish over the wall into the garden of Burlington House. Today's frontage, however, dates from 1911.

At the other end of the wall two identical pairs of shops were built in 1802 to flank the entrance to the courtyard of Albany (**E**). The existing frontage (**F**), quite unchanged since the engraving was published, was built in 1774 as a private house. In 1802 it was converted into chambers for bachelors to which were added two long blocks on either side of the garden at the back.

These were, and remain to this day, the most exclusive and desirable flats in London with a roster of residents which reads like a Who's Who of politics and the arts.

Piccadilly – South Side

OPPOSITE OLD BOND STREET stood the Egyptian Hall (**G**). This extraordinary building was designed for William Bullock, the naturalist and antiquarian, to house his museum of curiosities. It opened in 1812 and over the years became the centre for the most exotic exhibitions. 'General' Tom Thumb, the famous American dwarf, was probably its greatest single attraction. It was demolished in 1905 and 'Egyptian House' now marks the site where it once stood.

C   1896

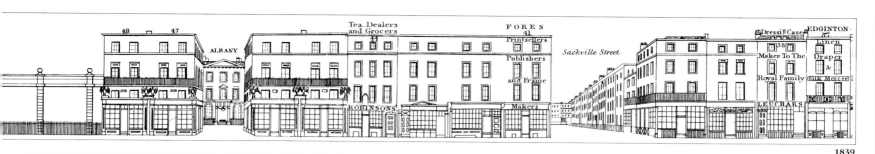

1839

E   1804

G   1842

F   1831

H   1904

One of the few buildings on the south side still standing is the Royal Institute of Painters in Water Colours (H) dating from 1883 though its street level has been totally redesigned.

Two great businesses remain today on their original sites which can be seen in Tallis's elevation below (I). No. 187 is Hatchards bookshop. John Hatchard opened his first bookshop where the Egyptian Hall later stood but in 1801 he moved to the site which the business still occupies. The original premises were rebuilt in 1909 with a shop-front clearly copied from that shown in Tallis's view.

The original Fortnum & Mason's is Nos. 182 and 183 in Tallis's view. The firm was founded in 1770 but these premises were built in 1835. The two buildings on either side were added later and the whole block rebuilt in 1928.

I *The south side of Piccadilly about 1839 shows a variety of shop fronts which include the original premises of Fortnum & Mason's and Hatchards.*

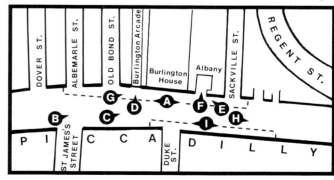

I   C1839

A

C1884

C

1885

D

1876

B

C1894

Piccadilly Circus 1

PICCADILLY CIRCUS (originally called Regent Circus) was created in 1819 by John Nash and formed part of his grand thoroughfare connecting Carlton House with Regent's Park. When this photograph (A) was taken, it was still just as Nash had conceived it and was a true circus as it appears in the old map. Behind the block on the left was Glasshouse Street followed immediately by Great Windmill Street. In Glasshouse Street was the entrance to the London Pavilion Music Hall which, at this time, was little more than a roofed-in stable yard. In the 1870s the Metropolitan Board of Works decided to create a new street connecting Piccadilly with Bloomsbury. This necessitated the demolition of the entire block on the left of the first photograph, and the pencil drawing (C) which was made by J. P. Emslie on 29 July 1885 shows the demolition in progress.

The new street (Shaftesbury Avenue) cut through the old London Pavilion which had to be rebuilt. The first stone was laid on 18 May 1885 and, by the time Emslie was making his sketch, the familiar triangular pediment of the new building could just be seen over the top of the demolished buildings on the right. With the demolition of the old block, and the formation of the new street, Piccadilly Circus was a true circus no more.

So complete was the transformation that it is difficult to believe that both photographs (A) and (B) were taken from exactly the same spot. On the right of each photo, the corner building will be seen to be identical. This is the block on the right of photograph (D), taken in 1876, showing the Criterion Theatre and Restaurant which had opened three years before. Completely gutted in 1990, the façade has been preserved.

A *Piccadilly Circus before 1885.*

B *The same view after the making of Shaftesbury Avenue. Eros is on the far left.*

C *The demolition of 1885.*

D *The Criterion in 1876, the façade of which remains today.*

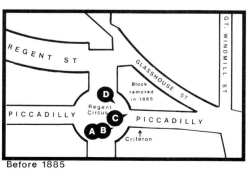

Before 1885

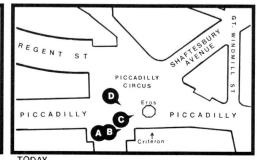

TODAY

A   C1862

Piccadilly Circus 2

IN WHAT IS ONE of the oldest 'instantaneous' photographs of Piccadilly Circus, taken in the 1860s **(A)**, the County Fire Office dominates the scene. This was built in 1819 and designed by Robert Abraham, although the founder of the company, Barber Beaumont, claimed that he designed the building himself. The figure of Britannia on the roof was the work of J. G. Bubb who used as his model Sophia Sarah Beaumont, the beautiful wife of the founder. When it was demolished in 1924 there was a public outcry but it was agreed that the new building successfully reflected the spirit of its predecessor. The familiar arches were back and a new Britannia (the old one having crumpled to dust) once more looked down Lower Regent Street.

B   C1863

C

C1865

Nash's Quadrant curving up Regent Street (**B**) is still beautiful despite the removal in 1848 of his original pillared colonnades projecting over the pavements because they were said to attract all sorts of vice after dark. (**C**) The two shops between the County Fire Office and the block later removed for Shaftesbury Avenue are in Glasshouse Street. Bennett's has long been swept away, but Van Raalte, Cigar Importer, was to survive well into the 1980s. It can be seen on the left of the photograph below (**D**) taken in 1910. This also shows the earliest electric signs, which were to become such a feature of the Circus. 'Mellin's Food' was probably the one put up first.

A & C *Old photographs of Piccadilly Circus show the original County Fire Office.*

B *Nash's Quadrant sweeping northward from the Circus in the 1860s.*

D *Buildings on Shaftesbury Avenue corner now covered with advertising signs.*

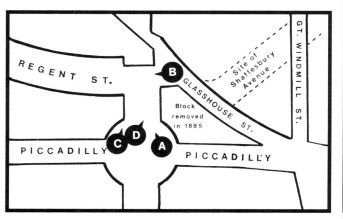

D

1910

A   1830

B   1909

C   1914

Coventry Street to Leicester Square

Looking back to Piccadilly Circus from virtually the same viewpoint, firstly in 1830 (A) and then in 1909 (B), the triangular block in the middle of the old engraving almost obscures the features common to both pictures, Swan & Edgar's and the old County Fire Office. The engraving (A) shows the corner shop of Joseph Egg, the famous gunsmith, who claimed to have invented the percussion cap. The removal of the triangular block opened up the view to show all Nash's original buildings and the majestic sweep of his Quadrant before they were all demolished in the 1920s. Eros, erected in 1893 and since shifted many times, is here seen on its original site.

Not only do these buildings (C) no longer exist but the turning on the left, Arundell Street, has also gone. However, on the far right of the photograph, taken in 1914, can just be seen the still-standing façade of the old Lyons Corner House, built in 1907, which was extended westwards in 1921 to cover the whole of this site. The shop is Lambert's, Goldsmiths and Silversmiths, whose frontage had not changed since the business was founded in 1800.

The north side of Leicester Square in 1907 (D) is easily recognizable today with the exception of Stagg & Mantle, the drapers, whose premises were rebuilt in 1938. Next door, the Empire Theatre has a frontage strangely similar to the present one. By its side is the palatial Queen's Hotel, opened in 1897, and beyond that the Hotel de l'Europe, built a year later, both standing today hardly altered.

The Empire, the most famous rendezvous for the Edwardian man-about-town, not only for its spicy productions but for its notorious promenade, was demolished in 1927 and rebuilt as a cinema.

The statue of Shakespeare (E) in 1874, the year it was erected and when the gardens, as yet treeless, were opened. The building on the left is Archbishop Tenison's school, where Hogarth's house once stood.

The Alhambra (F) just before it was gutted by fire in 1882. It was rebuilt retaining the old façade but in 1936 was completely demolished, together with the house adjoining on the north, and replaced by the present Odeon Cinema. The small house, seen on the left of the photograph, is the oldest surviving building in the square and today it has the Odeon as its neighbour.

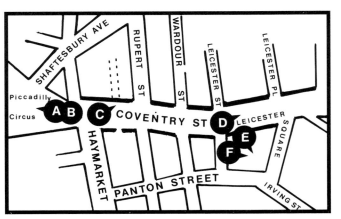

A *Looking back to Piccadilly Circus in 1830 with the shop of Joseph Egg the famous gunsmith.*

B *The same view in 1909 after the removal of the buildings in the centre. The dome belongs to the Piccadilly Hotel. Eros arrived in 1893.*

C *Not only has this shop on the corner of Arundell Street been demolished, but the street itself has been built over.*

D *Leicester Square in 1907 shows the Empire at the height of its fame.*

E *The statue of Shakespeare was put up when the gardens were laid out in 1874. The chimney comes from St Margaret's Baths in Orange Street.*

F *The Alhambra Theatre before the fire of 1882.*

D   1907

E   1874

F   C1880

A   1883

A *In this pencil drawing made in 1883, the gap between the buildings is recognizable today. This once led to Burford's Panorama but later became the entrance to the Roman Catholic church which still exists, as does the building next door, also seen in the photo below.*

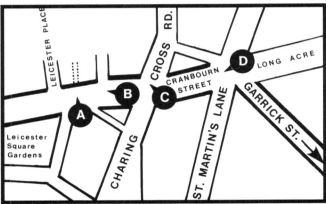

Daly's Theatre

THE SITE WHERE THE Warner Cinema now stands was previously occupied by Daly's Theatre, and before that by a row of shops **(A)** seen in the view (left) drawn by J. P. Emslie. These were all demolished except for the building on the left which can also be seen in the photograph below and which still stands today. Beside it is the entrance to what was once Barker's Panorama (later Burford's). This was a circular building specially designed for the exhibition of panoramas and it was opened in 1793 with 'A View of the Grand Fleet'. It was the world's first panorama rotunda and enjoyed enormous success, exhibiting a total of 126 different panoramas from its opening until 1863 when it closed its doors. The site was rebuilt as a Roman Catholic church (completely circular following the plan of the rotunda) which still exists with a new entrance in Leicester Place.

Daly's Theatre **(B)** was built for the American impresario Augustin Daly and opened on 27 June 1893. Its enormous popularity was largely due to the manager George Edwardes who put on those sparkling Victorian musical comedies whose names are remembered even today like *A Gaiety Girl, San Toy* (playing when the photo below was taken in 1900), *The Geisha* and *The Merry Widow*. It closed in 1937, was bought by Warner Brothers and rebuilt as the West End showcase for their films. It opened the following year with Errol Flynn's *Adventures of Robin Hood*.

B   1900

C

1902

B *Daly's Theatre in 1900. The home of Victorian and Edwardian London's most sparkling musical comedies, it was the last of the Leicester Square theatres to succumb to the popularity of the movies and closed in 1937. Rebuilt as a super-cinema, it opened in 1938 as The Warner.*

C *The London Hippodrome was built as a circus in 1900 and, although converted into a theatre-restaurant in 1957, the outside has hardly changed. It still retains its famous sky-line chariot as a reminder of its original function.*

D *This wood engraving of Cranbourne Street, one of a series of 'London Improvements' published in* The Illustrated London News, *dates from 1845 but the buildings on the left are immediately recognizable although the corner was slightly altered and a storey added in 1851. The architect was William Herbert.*

London Hippodrome

A THEATRE WITH QUITE a different character was the London Hippodrome (**c**). It was built for Edward Moss between 1899 and 1900 to provide 'a circus show second to none in the world, combined with elaborate stage spectacles impossible in any other theatre.' The circus arena could be lowered hydraulically to provide a tank holding 100,000 gallons (454,000 litres) of water for aquatic performances. London had seen nothing quite like the shows before. Red Indians shot down rapids in canoes, a one-legged cyclist plunged into the tank from 70 feet (21 metres), twenty elephants slid down a steep incline into the water and seventy polar bears appeared in a show called *The Arctic*. The novelty of the circus soon wore off, however, and in 1909 the arena became part of the auditorium. Circus gave way to opera and ballet and it was here that English audiences saw *Swan Lake* for the first time. In 1912 Albert de Courville's *Hello Ragtime!* was the first of his long series of successful revues and after 1926 the Hippodrome became famous for its musical comedies. It never suffered the fate of the other Leicester Square theatres in becoming a cinema but in 1957 it was converted into a cabaret-restaurant called Talk of the Town. Its exterior has hardly changed and it still retains the sky-line chariot symbolizing its circus origin.

Cranbourne Street

A MONG THE METROPOLITAN IMPROVEMENTS of the 1840s was a new thoroughfare connecting Coventry Street with Long Acre. This last section is all that remains, clearly recognizable today, although a storey was added in 1851, six years after this engraving appeared.

D

1845

A 1839

B C1830

A *King Street in 1839 from Tallis's street elevations.*

B *The view of Covent Garden from the end of King Street.*

C *Fowler's market buildings spoilt by Victorian additions.*

D *The handsome portico of St Paul's Church in 1792.*

E *Evan's Grand Hotel, the first hotel in England. Built in 1717, it still stands.*

F *The west front and entrance to St Paul's Church from the churchyard.*

C C1890

D   1792

Covent Garden

KING STREET WAS LAID OUT IN 1633 but nothing of this early period remains. However, a few buildings date from the late eighteenth century and can be identified in Tallis's elevation (A). Almost unchanged are No. 36 whose present frontage dates from 1751 and No. 37 which was built in 1774. At the end of King Street the vista of Covent Garden Market opens up (B). The first mention of a market here is in 1654 but in 1830 the casual assortment of shanty-stalls and sheds gave place to the handsome market buildings designed by Charles Fowler which we see today. The Victorians added all sorts of cast-iron excrescences (C) but after the market was closed and transferred to Nine Elms in the 1970s, these were all removed and the buildings restored to their original appearance although the interior was redeveloped into a pleasure complex of shops and restaurants.

St Paul's Church, seen here in 1792 (D), was built by Inigo Jones in 1631. The portico, renowned as the opening set for Shaw's *Pygmalion*, is really a sham with a false door against which, this being the east end, the altar is sited. The real entrance was at the west end, approached from the churchyard, seen here in 1766 (F).

Beyond St Paul's Church can be seen Lord Archer's House, the front of which is easily recognizable today. It was built in 1717 as a private house but in 1774 became a hotel, the first in England. Called the Grand, it remained a hotel until the 1880s (E). As Evan's Supper Rooms it was an early music hall and the Player's Theatre was once here.

E   1840

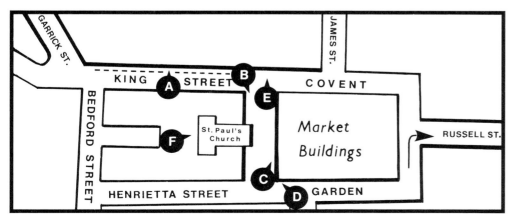

F   1766

A *The house of Tom Davies the bookseller where James Boswell first met Dr Johnson.*

B *No. 1 Russell Street was built in 1776 and was a chemist's shop in 1809.*

C *The Theatre Royal, Drury Lane, in 1813, the fourth and present building.*

D *By 1828 a portico has been added to the frontage.*

E *The present Royal Opera House with the Floral Hall next to it.*

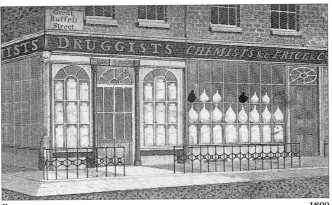

B   1809

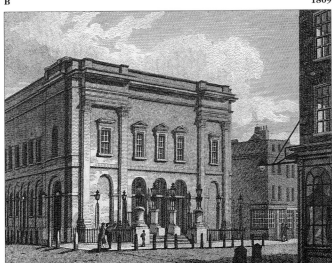

C   1813

D   1828

E   C1851

A   1836

Russell Street

No. 8, BUILT IN 1760 and carefully renovated (A), will go down in history as the bookshop of Tom Davies where, on 16 May 1763, James Boswell first met Dr Johnson. Davies, knowing how much Johnson disliked the Scots, mischievously introduced Boswell as a Scotsman. 'I do indeed come from Scotland', said the embarrassed Boswell, 'but I cannot help it.' 'That Sir', growled back Johnson, 'I find, is what a great many of your countrymen cannot help.'

No. 1 dates from 1776 and the corner shop was occupied by Price, the Chemist, in 1809 when he published this advertisement (B).

The same shop is seen on the right of the view of Drury Lane Theatre (C) with its somewhat squashed elevation drawn in 1813.

The theatre looks more familiar after its portico was added in 1820 (D). Apart from the colonnade of Ionic pillars along its left-hand side, added in 1831, the theatre looks much the same today.

Also unchanged is the façade of the Royal Opera House (E), which was designed by E. M. Barry and opened in 1858. The Floral Hall next door dates from 1860 but its semicircular glass roof was destroyed by fire in 1956.

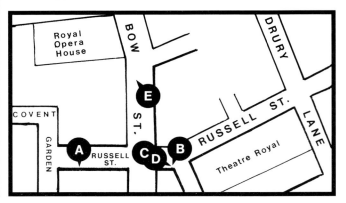

MARBLE ARCH TO
TOTTENHAM COURT ROAD

ABOVE *Approaching Oxford Circus in the 1890s.*

W E BEGIN WHERE London once ended. At this lonely extremity stood Tyburn gallows, as far out of town as you could get before open country was reached. The gallows, near Marble Arch, gave the name Tyburn Way to the thoroughfare we are walking but, as the main route out of London to the west, it was soon called Oxford Street, a name confirmed by the coincidence of the Earl of Oxford buying up tracts of land to the north for building development in the eighteenth century. Before then houses had appeared only on the south side – northwards was open country with uninterrupted views of Hampstead and Highgate.

It was originally residential but, after John Nash sliced it in half by cutting his Regent Street through the middle of it, its character changed rapidly. The elegant shops of Regent Street spilled out from the Circus, and Oxford Street became a shopping thoroughfare. These were humble shops at first, but with the coming of the twentieth century huge emporia began to appear. The great stores with household names like Mappin & Webb, Waring & Gillow are no more. Their handsome buildings still stand, proud tributes to Edwardian prosperity, but unhappily their ground floors, once elegant shops, have been debased into tatty boutiques. But with famous stores like D. H. Evans, John Lewis and Peter Robinson still with us to carry on the tradition of quality, Oxford Street remains the most famous street in London for clothes shopping. And towering above all in size and fame is Selfridges, solid and monumental, looking the same now as when it was completed in 1928. Only its famous window displays change, a veritable art gallery of window dressing.

Not all of Oxford Street is worthy of its fashionable past. Progressing eastwards beyond the Circus it becomes more and more down-market and by the time Tottenham Court Road is reached any sense of style or elegance has been abandoned to cheap clothes bazaars and blaring discos.

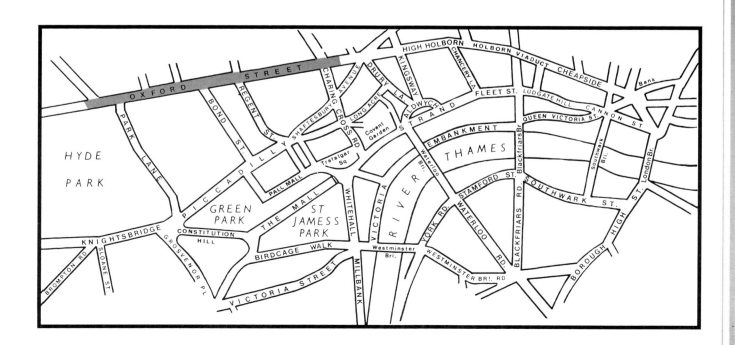

A *Tyburn Turnpike in 1813. Oxford Street is straight ahead and Edgware Road is on the left. The notorious gallows, Tyburn Tree, stood here until 1759.*

B *Marble Arch about 1912.*

C *View from opposite Marble Arch in about 1883 showing the outbuildings of Somerset House on the north corner of Park Lane on the right.*

A   1813

Tyburn Turnpike

'THE IMPRESSION MADE upon the mind of a traveller on his first visit to the metropolis of England depends, in no considerable degree, upon the road by which he makes his entrée. The entrance through Tyburn Turnpike may be considered the grandest passage into our immense metropolis: for although Piccadilly is adorned on the north side with nobler mansions, and on the south side with St James's Park; yet Oxford Street, from its uniform breadth, its commodious and spacious foot-way, and great extent, being one mile and a quarter in length, justly claims the pre-eminence, and is allowed to be one of the finest streets in Europe.' So read the text accompanying this view, which appeared in Ackermann's Repository, 1813.

B

C   C1883

This junction of Edgware Road and Oxford Street had been dominated by the notorious triple-tree of Tyburn gallows until 1759 when it was removed and the little toll-house built on its site. It remained here until 1829.

Marble Arch

THIS HANDSOME LANDMARK, so familiar to us in its present position, stood originally in front of Buckingham Palace. Designed by John Nash and erected at a cost of £75,000 in 1830, it lost its function as royal entry when Buckingham Palace was re-fronted and was demolished in 1848. Its numbered stones languished behind an enclosure in Green Park until 1851 when they were reassembled on the present site. At first it was truly a gateway to Hyde Park standing level with the park railings, but in 1908, owing to the increased congestion of traffic at this point, the railings were set back 180 feet leaving Marble Arch isolated on its island.

Park Lane Meets Oxford Street

THE UNTIDY CLUTTER of buildings and chimneys on the right (c) belong to a great mansion at the north end of Park Lane called Somerset House. The low building with three windows (seen in all three pictures) is the stable block behind its yard. Somerset House, where Warren Hastings the Governor-General of India lived for eight years, dated back to 1770 and was demolished in 1915. The opportunity was taken to widen Park Lane and the whole site was redeveloped as blocks of flats.

C1912

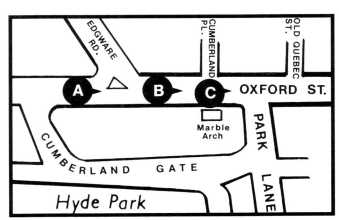

A

C1883

B   1921

C   1927

A *The Selfridges site in about 1883. Some of the Victorian buildings on the right, most notably the one on the corner of Duke Street, are still standing.*

B *By 1921 the first section of Selfridges had been built on the corner of Duke Street.*

C *Selfridges almost complete in 1927 except for the three Victorian buildings which had not yet been swallowed up.*

D *Looking back to the original Selfridges block on the corner of Duke Street. The corner building on the right still stands.*

E *The entrance to Stratford Place in 1815. One of the watch-houses, surmounted by a Coade stone lion, still survives.*

F *Looking towards Oxford Circus about 1894. Everything has been rebuilt with the exception of the small double-windowed frontage directly below the flag on the right.*

The Evolution of Selfridges

WHEN THE AMERICAN, Gordon Selfridge, decided to build 'the world's most beautiful store' in London, he chose as its site a block in Oxford Street between Duke Street and Orchard Street. Even Selfridge realized that his great vision could not be achieved all at once and as a first stage he acquired the numbers 398 to 422 which he described as 'a crowded mass of ill-consorted shops and houses' **(A)**. The first section, beginning on the corner of Duke Street **(B)**, was opened on 15 March 1909. The battles he fought with landlords and owners as he expanded westwards were gradually won and in 1925 he completed the Orchard Street end of his block with a gap still to be filled in the middle **(C)**. It was not until 1929 that he closed the gap with the monumental entrance dominated by the polychrome 'Queen of Time' clock which is such a feature today.

D   1922

E   1815

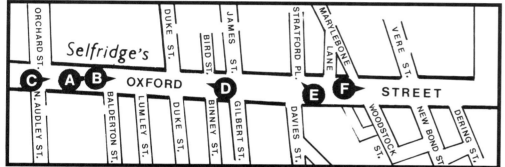

Stratford Place

STRATFORD PLACE is a cul-de-sac built in 1775 with many of its original houses still standing. The corner blocks, however, have been rebuilt (the western one closely following the original) so that all that remains today from this view (E), published in 1815, is the little stone lion on the right-hand watch-house. He was constructed of Coade's artificial stone and cost four guineas.

F   C1894

A   C1888

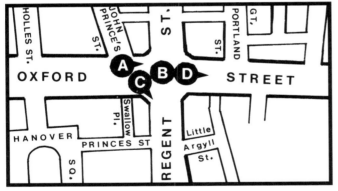

Oxford Circus

JOHN NASH WOULD have had no trouble in recognizing in these Victorian photographs the circus he created in the 1820s in spite of the ugly additions to the skyline. He knew it as Regent Circus, a name it shared with Piccadilly Circus until the 1880s when public confusion forced officialdom to adopt the name that cabbies and bus conductors had been using for years. Oxford Circus was dominated by large drapery shops and stores. One of the oldest, established in 1841, was Jay's Mourning Warehouse (on the right of **(C)**), a business created for the express purpose of catering to the bereaved. In the days of huge families, the demand for mourning black was insatiable and Jay's did not monopolize the field for long. Rival Mourning Warehouses sprang up including

B   C1889

C   **C1888**

Peter Robinson's opposite. This shop was known as Black Peter Robinson's to distinguish it from their original store on the north side of Oxford Street.

Peter Robinson's, seen in (**B**) under the flag, were later to engulf the whole of this north-east block on Oxford Circus. Their Regent Street shop (**c**) expanded upwards by adding an additional storey. Next to them, on the left, is the corner shop of Madame Louise, 'The Finest Milliner in Europe', who derived considerable publicity by persuading actresses like Sarah Bernhardt to wear her creations on stage.

Further on down Regent Street two circular buildings flank the entrance to Little Argyll Street. The nearer of the two is a reasonable copy of Nash's original building which was burnt down in 1830. This was the Argyll Rooms, famous for concerts and assemblies. The other circular building was soon to be taken over by Dickins & Jones who are still on the same site today although, in common with everything else in the photograph, their premises have been rebuilt. In fact they were the first to go in the great Regent Street rebuilding after World War I.

A *The busy approach to Oxford Circus in about 1888.*

B *This photograph clearly shows the absolute symmetry of Nash's original circus. Unfortunately since the buildings were first erected in the 1820s a mess of tatty roof additions has been allowed to ruin the skyline.*

C *Looking down Regent Street from Oxford Circus in the 1880s.*

D *The eastern half of Oxford Street from the Circus. All that remains today is the building with the three pointed windows on the skyline above the waggon on the right. It is also evident in photograph (**A**). It was built in 1887.*

D   **C1890**

A   1908

The East End of Oxford Street

THE ELEGANT NEW PREMISES of Mappin & Webb were only two years old when this photograph (**A**) was taken in 1908. The building still stands, the ground floor a poor travesty of its original splendour. Its neighbour to the west was Waring & Gillow (**B**), built 1901-5 in a swaggering baroque style. The handsome façade exists today but in 1977 the street level was destroyed in a squalid commercial development.

Oxford Street has lost all the places of entertainment for which it was once noted. The oldest was the Pantheon (**C**). Opened in 1773 for balls, masquerades, concerts etc., it was enormously popular, but it gradually declined until in 1867 it was bought by Gilbey's as a wine store (**D**). They sold it to Marks & Spencer in 1937 who rebuilt it as it is today with the name 'Pantheon' on the skyline. The Princess's Theatre in the photograph (**E**) dated from 1881, its predecessor having been burnt down. Never very successful, it closed in 1902. It was demolished in 1931 to be replaced by a Woolworth's store and in 1978 it became a shopping complex called Oxford Walk. Greatest of all was the Oxford Music Hall (**F**) seen here after its rebuilding in 1892. On its opening night Marie Lloyd topped the bill singing 'Oh Mr Porter'. In 1926 it was demolished and a Lyons Corner House built on the site (see p. 42).

B   1912

C   1831

D   1880S

F   C1900

E   1896

A *Mappin & Webb in 1908 and (**B**) in 1912 with Waring & Gillow.*

C *The Pantheon in 1831.*

D *The Pantheon used as a wine store.*

E *The Princess's Theatre in 1896.*

F & G *The Oxford Music Hall in its Victorian heyday and being demolished in 1926.*

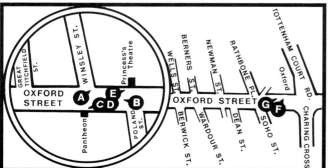

G   1926

St Giles Circus

THE PHOTOGRAPH ON THE RIGHT (A), looking west along Oxford Street, was taken in August 1884. The tall block covered in posters was an island on the corner of Tottenham Court Road. Behind it ran a curious little passage called Bozier's Court which, because of the pub on its corner, was nicknamed 'Boozer's Alley'. This block had for years been threatened with demolition, and in 1893 the West End Clothiers' Company, anticipating its removal, built one of their super-stores behind it in Bozier's Court. In 1900 the block was at last demolished and the new clothing store was revealed. A little further along Oxford Street is a building with a projecting clock. This is the old Oxford Music Hall, originally built by Charles Morton in 1861, and demolished in 1892. On the left is Crown Street, soon to be swept away to form Charing Cross Road.

This photograph (B) was taken at the same time as the preceding one but the camera has now swung to the right to take the view looking north up Tottenham Court Road. On the left is the same island block that appears in the other picture and the first turning on the left is the other end of Bozier's Court. On the right is the entrance to Meux's Brewery, one of the largest in London covering nearly four acres, and just beyond this is the still-existing Horseshoe, grown from a modest tavern into an enormous restaurant (table d'hôte 3s/6d) with its huge horseshoe-shaped dining table. Sandwiched between the Horseshoe and the brewery gate was, in 1914, one of London's early cinemas, the Court Electric Theatre. It was the forerunner of the mammoth Dominion which arose in 1929 on the site of the old brewery.

By 1902, when this double photograph was taken (C), the obtrusive island block had been removed, revealing the large clothing store behind it. This still stands almost unaltered. In Oxford Street is the new frontage of the rebuilt Oxford Music Hall now with a side entrance in Tottenham Court Road seen directly under the tip of the flag. In 1926 it was replaced by one of Lyons great Corner Houses. The building on the left, looking much the same today, marks the beginning of Charing Cross Road, opened in 1887.

A & B *Looking along Oxford Street and Tottenham Court Road. Both photographs were taken in August 1884.*

C *The same view some eighteen years later.*

A

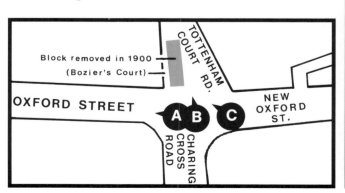

C

1884 B

1884

1902

A   C1904

New Oxford Street

FOR HUNDREDS OF YEARS, any traffic travelling along Oxford Street to Holborn would have to turn right on reaching the bottom of Tottenham Court Road and continue along St Giles High Street. This ancient route cut through St Giles 'Rookery', a notorious slum area. In the 1840s it was decided to avoid this by making a direct route and New Oxford Street (A) was created. It was finished in 1847 but nothing remains of the original buildings.

The curious cast-iron and glass structure (B) is actually one of the earliest telephone kiosks to appear in the streets of London, dating from about 1903. Apparently a coin in the slot gave the caller access to the telephone inside the box. Illuminated at night, its posters advertised the Great Central Railway.

A *Looking east along New Oxford Street.*
B *One of London's first*

telephone kiosks on the corner of Charing Cross Road.

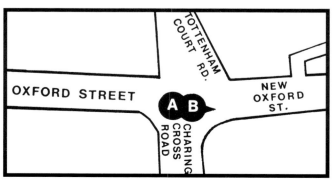

B   C1904

HOLBORN TO THE BANK

ABOVE *The Royal Exchange about 1900.*

OLBORN, THE MOST northerly of London's ancient highways, can boast, appropriately, one of London's most ancient buildings, the half-timbered Tudor frontage of Staple Inn, looking today much as Shakespeare must have known it. Facing it, an architectural treasure of quite a different kind – Waterhouse's red-brick Gothic Prudential building – happily survives despite the extensive rebuilding here which destroyed Gamage's huge department store, known as the poor man's Harrods.

Holborn Circus, presided over by Prince Albert in army uniform, incongruously raising his cocked hat, leads straight on to one of Victorian London's greatest engineering triumphs, Holborn Viaduct, which displaced thousands of slum houses and cost as much to build as the Houses of Parliament. The copper dome of the Old Bailey topped by its figure of Justice, carrying scales but without a blindfold, still dominates the skyline here in spite of all the high buildings around it.

A slight diversion northwards past the City's largest church, St Sepulchre's, brings us to Smithfield and London's oldest church, St Bartholomew the Great. Then we turn back along Newgate Street, reminding us of the grim prison which stood on the site of the Old Bailey, and on to the area north of St Paul's dedicated to the postal service since the Penny Post, once busy with mail coaches and now a traffic gyratory system.

Cheapside, almost entirely rebuilt after its destruction in the war, has its splendidly restored church of St Mary-le-Bow, within the sound of whose bells all cockneys are born.

Which brings us to the very heart of the City, an exciting spot where seven major thoroughfares converge, and where the Bank of England, the Royal Exchange, the Mansion House and all the other great commercial buildings merge in perfect harmony in spite of their different periods: a harmony which will hopefully survive if the excesses of modern planning can be curbed.

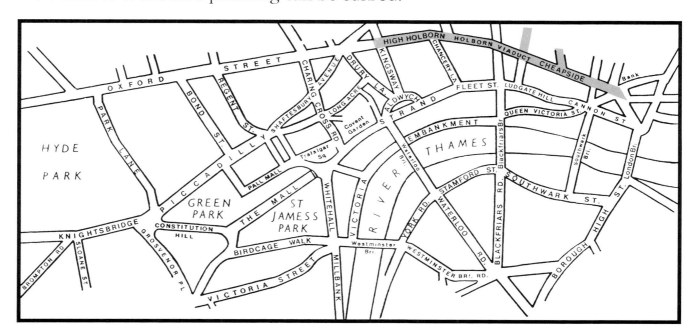

A   C1880

High Holborn

WHEN KINGSWAY WAS OPENED IN 1905 this view (A) looking eastwards along High Holborn was transformed. All the buildings in the foreground as far back as the lamp manufacturers on the corner of King's Gate Street were demolished and most of the others rebuilt.

There has been a wedge of buildings (B) between High Holborn and the narrow alleyway on the left called Little Turnstile, which leads to Lincoln's Inn Fields, for well over 300 years. The end building, dating from 1907, still dominates the scene today. To its left is the Holborn Empire (C), the third music hall on this site, the first having been built in 1857. This building, opened in 1906, was damaged in the blitz and pulled down in 1960. The men's lavatory was swept away when the new traffic system was created here and it will be sadly missed by its many patrons who have fond memories of its glass water cisterns in which the attendant kept goldfish.

B   1912

C   1907

D   C1900

The entrance to Gray's Inn (D), bounded by enough pubs to satisfy all its lawyers, can be seen just behind the bracket clock belonging to Henekey's, the only pub still existing although its name has been changed to the *Cittie of York*.

For centuries a long narrow block of houses called Middle Row stuck out into the road just west of Holborn Bars (E). (Holborn Bars was once an actual barrier barring the entrance to the City. Later it was replaced by two stone obelisks marking the City boundary. One of these, still standing, can be seen in all the last three pictures.) Middle Row, as early as 1657, was referred to as 'a mighty hinderance to Holborn', but it was not until 1867 that it was finally demolished.

At that time the street frontage of Staple Inn was covered in stucco which was removed towards the end of the last century revealing the wonderful Elizabethan half-timbering we see today (F).

E   1867

F   C1907

The building jutting out on the left (**G**) is the Prudential Assurance building designed by Alfred Waterhouse in 1879. Next to it is the classical façade of Furnival's Inn, a block of residential chambers where Charles Dickens lived and wrote *Pickwick Papers*. In 1898 it was demolished and the Prudential, having bought the freehold ten years before, extended their premises over its site, again commissioning Waterhouse as architect. The result was the huge terracotta masterpiece happily still standing.

A *The west end of High Holborn, demolished to make Kingsway.*

B *The Edwardian block on the left still stands.*

C *The Holborn Empire, demolished in 1960.*

D *The pub on the left is now called the* Cittie of York.

E *Middle Row drawn just before it was removed.*

F *Staple Inn remains as London's finest example of Elizabethan domestic architecture.*

G *Looking east along Holborn.*

G   C1896

B   C1902

C   C1920

D   1907

A   1884

Gamage's and Holborn Circus

THE OLD BELL AT 123 HOLBORN (A) was a busy coaching inn in the days before the railways and was still running an occasional coach when this photograph was taken in 1884. But its days as a coaching inn were numbered and in 1898 it was rebuilt as the large Victorian public house and dining rooms seen sandwiched between the two Gamage's blocks (D). Albert Walter Gamage opened his first shop, No. 128, on the corner of Leather Lane, in 1878. He gradually spread eastwards until, at the end of the 1890s, he was able to build an entire block from Leather Lane to the Old Bell. Around the 1900s he began buying property on the other side of the Old Bell and his 'Great Extension' was being advertised when photograph (B) was taken, while (C) shows the same site after the extension had been built. The whole of Gamage's (D), including the original block, was demolished in the 1970s. In the distance is the completed Prudential Assurance building with its central tower finished in 1902. This photograph (E) was taken just after 1874 when the statue of Prince Albert was unveiled. On the right is the tower of St Andrew's Church (G) and in the distance is St Sepulchre's, Holborn. The tower partly obscured by the block on the right belongs to the City Temple.

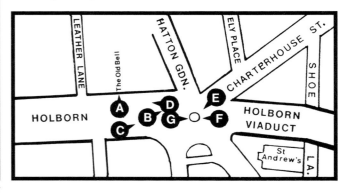

F   C1919

A *The Old Bell in 1884.*

B *The Circus end of Holborn with Gamage's advertising their 'Great Extension of Premises'.*

C *The same view after Gamage's had built their extension.*

D *Looking back to the Prudential Assurance building.*

E *Holborn Circus just after 1874 when Prince Albert's statue was erected.*

F & G *The completed circus, mostly destroyed in World War II.*

E   C1875

G   C1890

A   1864

A *Looking eastwards down Holborn Hill to the valley where the Fleet River once flowed and beyond to St Sepulchre's Church. This lithograph was copied from a photograph taken in 1864*

which is now too faded to be reproduced.

B *Holborn Viaduct roadway in the 1890s. Over the balustrade on the right is St Andrew's churchyard*

with Shoe Lane now far below running under the roadway. The building on the right is the City Temple.

Holborn Hill Becomes Holborn Viaduct

THE VIEWS ABOVE AND ABOVE RIGHT were taken from virtually the same position but whereas (A) was made from ground level before Holborn Viaduct was built (B), was made high up on the Viaduct roadway. Common to both pictures are the tower of St Sepulchre's Church in the distance, and the bushes on the right which mark the end of St Andrew's churchyard. In the first view we are looking down the steep descent of Holborn Hill to the valley where Holborn Bridge once crossed the River Fleet. This was covered over in the eighteenth century and Farringdon Street created. Its northern section, originally called Victoria Street, is the first turning on the left. Next comes the beginning of Snow Hill and Skinner Street leading to St

C   1804

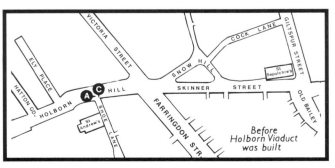

Before Holborn Viaduct was built

B   C1890

Sepulchre's Church. On the right is Shoe Lane and the brick wall of St Andrew's churchyard, seen more clearly in **(c)** where the slope of the road illustrates the steepness of Holborn Hill. It was this steepness, notoriously dangerous for horsedrawn vehicles, especially in winter, which prompted the creation of Holborn Viaduct. The first stone was laid in 1867 and it was opened by Queen Victoria on 6 November 1869, the same day that she opened Blackfriars Bridge. With the well-known iron bridge over Farringdon Street **(D)** virtually the only visible part of the Viaduct, it is difficult to realize that the complete structure is 1,400 feet (426 metres) long stretching from Holborn Circus to the Old Bailey. Its cost of over £2,000,000 included the creation of two new thoroughfares, Charterhouse Street and St Andrew's Street.

c *The church of St Andrew's Holborn from an aquatint published in 1804. The Viaduct roadway cut right across its churchyard, level with the top of the wall, necessitating the removal of*

12,000 bodies which were reburied at Ilford.

D *Here the Viaduct bridge crosses Farringdon Street. On the right is one of the four so-called 'step*

buildings' which incorporated staircases leading to Farringdon Street. This still stands, as does its companion out of the picture on the right.

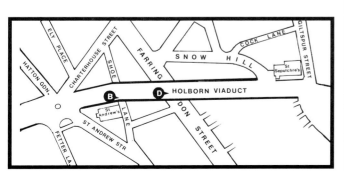

D   C1890

A C1880

B C1878

A *Looking west along Holborn Viaduct with the church of St Sepulchre's on the right and the City Temple in the distance.*

B *The Imperial Hotel on the corner of Old Bailey.*

C *The newly-built Newgate Prison.*

D *Newgate just before its demolition.*

E *The old prison demolished, with the dome of St Paul's in the distance.*

F *The Central Criminal Court or Old Bailey.*

G *Looking east along Newgate Street, the Viaduct Tavern on the left.*

The End of Holborn Viaduct

Looking west along Holborn Viaduct in the 1880s presents a scene which would remain unchanged until World War II (**A**). Surviving the blitz are the City Temple in the distance and St Sepulchre's on the right whose porch juts out in front of Snow Hill. Opposite is the Holborn Viaduct Hotel which was built in front of the London Chatham & Dover Railway terminus. The hotel was built in 1877 and destroyed by bombing in 1941. The new building gives open access to Holborn Viaduct Station. The ornate building next door (**B**) was also an hotel, The Imperial, and still stands today having survived both bombs and developers. Though now converted into offices, its old name is still recalled by the Imperial Eagle perched on one of the dormers in the middle of the roof.

Newgate Becomes the Old Bailey

The notorious Newgate Prison, originally part of the actual gate which spanned Newgate Street, was rebuilt in the 1770s (**C**) and, although badly damaged in the Gordon Riots of 1780, remained virtually unchanged (**D**) until its demolition in 1902 (**E**). It was outside the first doorway on the right that executions took place until 1868. In that year public executions were abolished and were thereafter conducted within the walls. On its site was built the Central Criminal Court or Old Bailey (**F**). With its dome a miniature version of St Paul's supporting the famous statue of Justice, it was opened by King Edward VII on 27 February 1907. The Viaduct Tavern (**G**), a typical Victorian pub dating from 1867, has cellars which are said to be the cells of old Newgate.

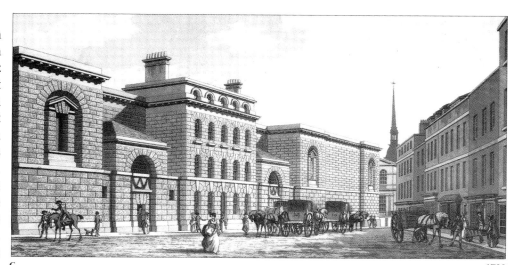

C   1799

D   1900

E   1902

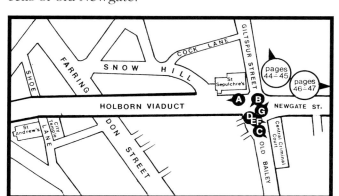

G   C1896

F   C1910

A   1896

Smithfield

Occupying THE WHOLE EAST SIDE is St Bartholomew's Hospital with its eighteenth-century gateway unaltered today (A). On the left is the circular ramp down which horse-drawn vehicles could reach the railway station beneath the market which linked up main lines for the transportation of meat all over the country. It was opened on 1 September 1871. Today cars drive down the ramp to the underground car park. In the middle of the circle a garden was built featuring an impressive drinking fountain (B) whose superstructure fell into disrepair and had to be taken down leaving only the charming statue of 'Peace'.

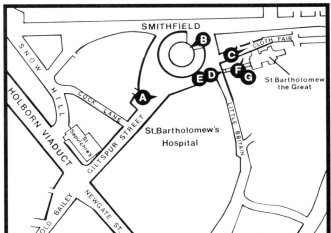

B   1870S   C   C1890

D
1837

F
1739

A *St Bartholomew's Hospital.*

B *The drinking fountain erected in 1873.*

C *Old houses in Cloth Fair.*

D *St Bartholomew's ancient entrance.*

E *The gatehouse before the half-timbering was revealed.*

F & G *St Bartholomew's churchyard changed little over the centuries.*

St Bartholomew The Great

WHAT WE SEE TODAY of London's oldest church is less than half the original building which, before the Reformation, actually faced on to Smithfield, and its original doorway became the still-existing archway to what is now the churchyard, but what was originally the nave. Over the medieval archway (D) a gatehouse was built in 1559 which looked quite undistinguished (E) until 1916 when a German bomb from a Zeppelin raid fell nearby, displacing the ugly tiles with which it was covered revealing the half-timbering we now see. Though 150 years separate the two views, above (F) and below (G), the only change appears to be the lowered footpath to the entrance in the tower which was made in 1865. On the left are the backs of the houses on the south side of Cloth Fair, removed about 1914. Some of the seventeenth-century houses on the north side of Cloth Fair (C) still exist greatly restored, while the projecting house on the right was replaced by the church's north porch in 1893.

E
C1900

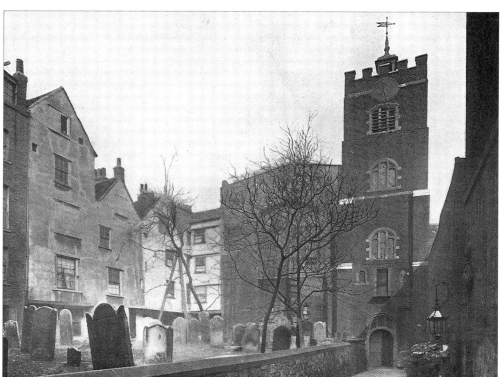

G
C1890

A

C1830

B

C1900

The General Post Office

For 150 years after the Great Fire, the headquarters of the Post Office was situated in a large private house in Lombard Street, but with the introduction of mail coaches the street became impossibly congested and unsuitable for its purpose. A two-acre space was cleared in the rookeries of St Martin's le Grand and a huge building, specially designed by Robert Smirke to meet the needs of the mail coach service, was erected on the site. This was the General Post Office, opened on 23 September 1829 (A and C). Ironically, in a few years, the coming of the railway would make the mail coach obsolete but the enormous growth of the postal service, especially after the introduction of the Uniform Penny Post, makes the story of the post office buildings one of continued expansion. In 1873 another huge block (D) was opened opposite the old building. Its corner can be seen on the right of (E) and it just appears on the left of (C). Above it, past the lamppost, is the third extension opened in 1895 to accommodate the Central Savings Bank. This building still stands although recently converted into offices. The only other building still recognizable in photograph (C) is the one with the small dome on the corner just above the omnibus.

Smirke's handsome building, whose portico framed a unique view of St Paul's (B), was closed in 1910 and its business transferred immediately to the new, and present, General Post Office in King Edward Street.

A *The newly-built Post Office in St Martin's le Grand. Opposite, the old Bull & Mouth inn has just been demolished. It was rebuilt a few years later.*

B *View of St Paul's through the portico of the General Post Office.*

C *Three post office buildings – GPO East on the right, with GPO West and North on the left.*

D *GPO West just after it had been built in 1873.*

E *Cheapside joining Newgate Street with GPO West on the right.*

C   C1895

D   C1873   E

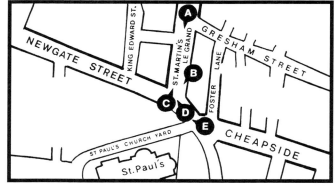

C1890

A   C1900

B   C1875

The Beginning of Cheapside

THIS BUSY JUNCTION, where Newgate Street meets Cheapside, has changed out of all recognition since it was bombed and rebuilt after the Second World War. The only point of reference in photograph (A) is the church of St Vedast, Foster Lane, whose spire appears above the rooftops. Today the whole church can be clearly seen from here. The view of St Paul's Cathedral (B) has also been opened up. The finely proportioned building on the right dated from the early nineteenth century but was rebuilt in 1900. The opposite block was also rebuilt about the same time and can be seen on the extreme right of (A). The statue is that of Sir Robert Peel. It was erected in 1855 and removed in 1939 because of traffic congestion, thus escaping the blitz which destroyed all the surrounding buildings.

A *The statue of Sir Robert Peel looks down Cheapside.*

B *In spite of post-war changes, the view of St Paul's is the same.*

C *Looking east along Cheapside.*

C   C1890

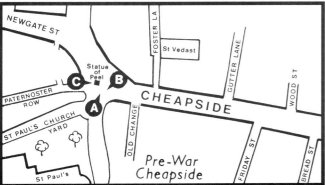

Pre-War Cheapside

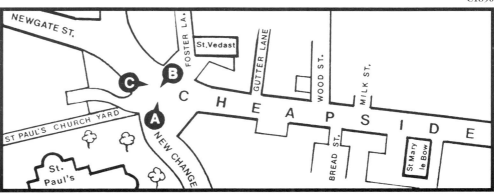

A   C1896

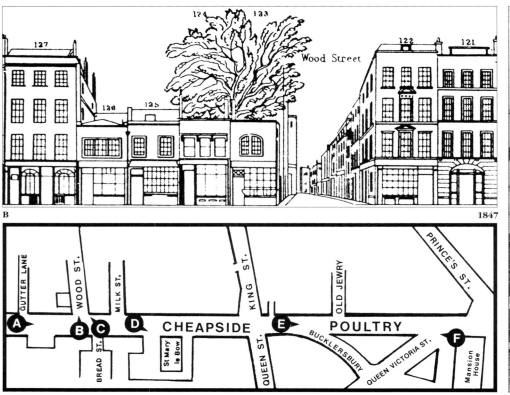

B   1847

C   1901

Cheapside

CHEAPSIDE SUFFERED TERRIBLY in the blitz and was almost totally destroyed. On the night of 29 December 1940 fire bombs fell and the flames spread rapidly when the City's water supply failed. All the buildings on the south side, with the happy exception of St Mary-le-Bow, were either completely destroyed or their tottering walls were later demolished to make way for modern developments. The north side suffered less and at least two Victorian buildings (those just behind the lamppost in (A)) still survive today. The tree, just beyond them, is still flourishing and marks one of the most remarkable survivals in the City. This venerable plane tree is growing in what was once the graveyard of St Peter Westchepe, a medieval church burnt down in the Great Fire of 1666. In 1401 the parishioners had obtained a licence to erect a row of small shops in front of their church. After the Great Fire the church was not rebuilt but the shops were (B and C) and here they still stand with the date of their erection, 1687, on a stone tablet on the back wall. They are the only surviving examples of the 'least sort of building' of two storeys authorized by the Post-Fire Rebuilding Act of 1667. Wren's beautiful church of St Mary-le-Bow has always had houses huddled up against it, as in the print (D) dated 1802, but now, with post-war Cheapside widened and opened up, it can be seen to greater advantage than ever before. In 1830, Bucklersbury (E), the narrow thoroughfare on the right, was twice as long as it is today. It was cut in half by the formation of Queen Victoria Street in the 1860s and, with Poultry on the north, created an important wedge of buildings which became the subject of intense architectural controversy in recent times.

A Cheapside in the 1890s.

B Four shops depicted by Tallis.

C The same shops, in 1901, still exist today.

D St Mary-le-Bow, 1802.

E Poultry, with Bucklersbury on the right.

F Poultry from the Mansion House.

D   1802

E   1830

F   C 1890

A   1   2   3   4   5   6

B   C1875

The Heart of the City

THE 'BANK CROSSING' as it is sometimes called has changed surprisingly little since the engraving (A1) was made in 1838. True, all these views now have backdrops of soaring office skyscrapers but there is enough of the past left to make every picture instantly recognizable. The Royal Exchange (B), the third on the same site, the others having been burnt down in 1666 and 1838, was opened by the young Queen Victoria in 1844 and has recently been given an additional storey without detracting from its appearance. Soane's Bank of England is on the left (see next page) while on the right are the handsome neo-classical offices designed by Philip Hardwick for the Globe Insurance Company in 1837, seen also in (A3). From the earliest times, the old Royal Exchanges were obscured behind a triangular wedge of houses, part of which can be seen in (A2). This was swept away in 1844 to give the new Exchange a clear forecourt on which was erected the equestrian statue of the Duke of Wellington (F). The sculptor was Francis Chantrey and, as with his statue of George IV in Trafalgar Square, the Duke is depicted riding without boots or saddle or stirrups. It was unveiled on 18 June 1844, the anniversary of the Battle of Waterloo.

The view along Poultry to St Mary-le-Bow in Cheapside (C, D and E) has seen some changes over the years and never more so than in the 1990s. In the eighteenth century, Dance's Mansion House, built in 1752, dominated the scene (C). The first transformation came in 1852 when the National Mercantile Assurance building was erected next to the Mansion House (D). It stood for barely twenty years and was demolished in 1870 to make way for Queen Victoria Street. On the acute corner created by the new street there arose the familiar and much-loved Mappin & Webb building designed by John Belcher (E). On the other side of Poultry (C and D) is Wren's church of St Mildred which was demolished in 1872 when this photograph (E) was taken.

1838

A *The view from the end of Prince's Street in 1838.*
1 Corner of the Bank of England. 2 Bank Buildings, a block which stood in front of the Royal Exchange until 1844. 3 Globe Insurance Company on the junction of Cornhill and Lombard Street. 4 The church of St Mary Woolnoth. 5 The Monument at the end of King William Street. 6 Nos. 1 – 4 Lombard Street. 7 Mansion House.

B *The Royal Exchange in the 1870s with the Bank of England on the left.*

C *The Mansion House looking west along Poultry with the church of St Mary-le-Bow in the distance and St Mildred on the right, in 1783.*

D *The same view in about 1863.*

E *The statue of Wellington, erected in front of the Royal Exchange in 1844.*

F   C1870

C   1783

D   C1863

E   1872

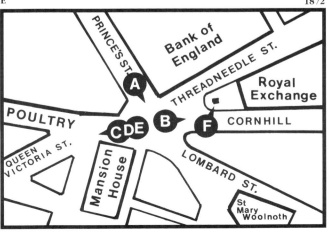

A   1798

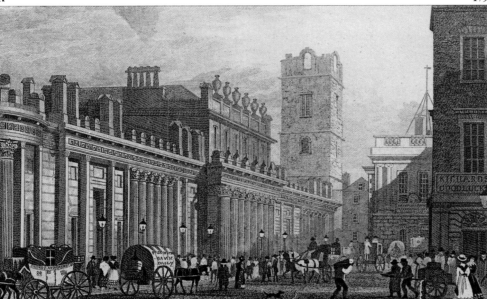

B   1827

D   C1875

The Bank of England

THE BANK OF ENGLAND had been in existence for forty years before the Governors decided to build permanent premises. The first building was opened on the Threadneedle Street site in 1734 but this soon became inadequate and two single-storey wings were added by Sir Robert Taylor as seen in the aquatint (A) dated 1798. When Sir John Soane was appointed architect he set about extending the building until it occupied the whole of the present three-acre site and the view (B) shows the south front in 1827 as rebuilt by Soane. In both prints the church in the background is St Bartholomew's, demolished in 1841, and jutting out on the right is the old Royal Exchange burnt down in 1838. The solidity of Soane's Bank inspired confidence for over 130 years and even when the interior was rebuilt and additional storeys added in the 1920s, Soane's massive outer walls were retained and remain virtually unchanged today.

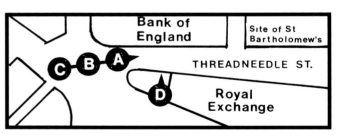

A   *The Bank of England, with the original block in the centre of the picture and Taylor's additional wings on either side.*

B   *The front as rebuilt by Sir John Soane. The church in the background is St Bartholomew's, demolished in 1841.*

C   *On the right is the present Royal Exchange, rebuilt after the fire of 1838.*

D   *Soane's curtain wall remains today in spite of the twentieth-century additions of Sir Herbert Barker.*

C   C1890

MILLBANK TO
ST JAMES'S STREET

ABOVE *Trafalgar Square at the beginning of the twentieth century.*

THIS WALK TAKES US through the Palace of Westminster. Today it is a palace in name only; once it was truly a royal palace, the official residence of all our kings, from Edward the Confessor to Henry VIII. Many of its ancient buildings existed until the fire of 1834 and even today Westminster Hall and the Jewel Tower survive from the Middle Ages. Always the administrative centre of the Kingdom, the Palace lost its identity when it was completely rebuilt by Barry and Pugin and became the Houses of Parliament. Here is Victorian Gothic at its most arrogant, particularly as it stands opposite a most beautiful example of the real thing, the Henry VII Chapel of Westminster Abbey.

The great open space of Parliament Square is now no more than a giant roundabout, defying the pedestrian to cross the road to the sculpture gallery of prime ministers in its centre, or to enjoy the views of Big Ben and the Abbey.

Whitehall, itself once a royal palace, is sturdily Edwardian with forbidding government offices, while No. 10 Downing Street lies inaccessible behind cast-iron gates. But it still has one architectural gem to offer, Inigo Jones's Banqueting House. It was through a window here that Charles I stepped on to the scaffold and his statue has been looking down to the spot from Charing Cross for 300 years. Charing Cross became Trafalgar Square where we turn left along Cockspur Street.

Here we are very much in the world of John Nash and at Waterloo Place we can appreciate the great triumphal route he planned for the Prince Regent, with our backs to where Carlton House once stood looking up to Piccadilly Circus where Regent Street sweeps around on its way to Regent's Park.

We go along Pall Mall to Henry VIII's red-brick palace of St James, a miniature Hampton Court, sitting at the angle where St James's Street turns up to Piccadilly. This is clubland, and once enjoyed a quiet air of dignified reserve; now it is a racetrack for one-way traffic, where the only peace is enjoyed by the club members secure behind their closed doors.

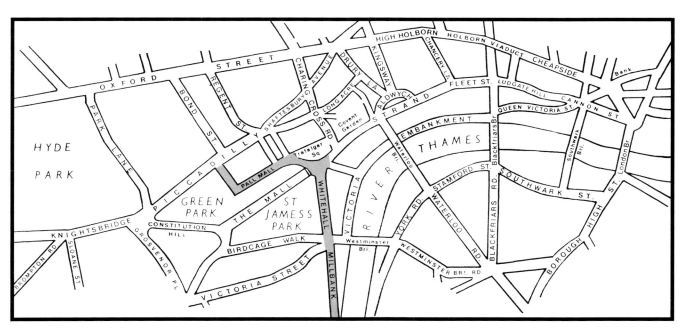

Victoria Tower. Westminster.

Millbank

THE PHOTOGRAPH ON THE LEFT (A), taken sometime in the early 1860s, shows the cluttered and somewhat unworthy approach from the south along Millbank to the recently built Victoria Tower of the new Houses of Parliament.

It graphically illustrates the extraordinary architectural contrasts which the Victorians were imposing on Georgian and Regency London at this time and emphasizes the dramatic impact which Sir Charles Barry's colossal tower must have had. At 336 feet (102 metres), it was the largest and tallest tower in the world when it was built, taller than any American skyscraper of the period. Barry designed it as a repository for state documents with a grand ceremonial royal entrance at ground level (two functions which it still serves), but he never lived to see it completed. The work was finished by his son Edward.

The pub jutting out on the left is the Portman Arms on the corner of Wood Street (now Great Peter Street) which was demolished in 1903, when the roadway was widened and the Church Commissioners' Office built. On the right are commercial buildings backing on to the Thames whose wharves can be seen in the other photograph (B). The first gap in the pavement leads down to the wharf of the Chartered Gas Company and the next leads to Dorset Wharf. In 1880 all the buildings and wharves between Dorset Wharf and the Victoria Tower were removed to make way for Victoria Tower Gardens, but it was not until 1912 that the rest of the buildings were demolished and the gardens enlarged to their present size.

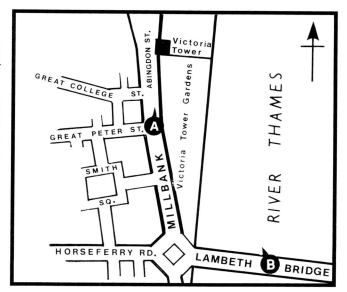

A *Millbank in the 1860s looking north to the Victoria Tower. Just beyond the pub on the left Millbank becomes Abingdon Street.*

B *The Millbank wharves from Lambeth Bridge before the foreshore was reclaimed and Victoria Tower Gardens were laid out in 1880.*

B

Old Palace Yard

A   **1860S**

THE ENORMOUS BULK of the Victoria Tower dominates this view of Abingdon Street in the 1860s (**A**). The drawing (**B**) made in 1847 shows it being built with the remains of the old Palace of Westminster, burnt down in 1834, in the background. Common to both views is the pub on the right called the Chequers. This, together with its neighbouring houses down to Dorset Wharf, were demolished in 1880 to make way for the first part of Victoria Tower Gardens. The row of Georgian houses on the left lasted much longer and was not pulled down until 1943 after some bomb damage. The only survivor is the one in the centre of photograph (**C**). Their removal opened up a view which revealed the charming little Jewel Tower, built in 1365 for Edward III, that for centuries had been completely engulfed by later buildings and almost obscured from view (**E, F** and **G**). More houses on the west side of Old Palace Yard obstructed the view of Westminster Abbey throughout the eighteenth century (**D**) while a group of Government buildings, including the Ordnance Office, to the north of the Henry VII Chapel hid St Margaret's Church. Facing Henry VII Chapel across the road is part of the Law Courts described on page 71.

B   **1847**

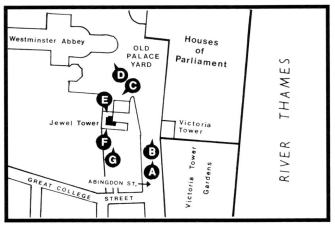

A *Abingdon Street with the newly-built Victoria Tower.*

B *Ruins of the Old Palace of Westminster with Victoria Tower being built.*

C *Georgian houses on the west side of Old Palace Yard.*

C   **1890S**

D 1793

E 1805

F 1805

G 1900S

D *Aquatint of Old Palace Yard from Malton's* Picturesque Tour *dated 1793 showing the houses which obscured Westminster Abbey. The one on the left is on the corner of Abingdon Street. Immediately to its right is the same house seen on the right of photograph* **(C)**.

E *and* **F** *Engravings from Smith's* Antiquaries of Westminster *showing the Jewel Tower hemmed in by buildings.*

G *The Jewel Tower was not easily accessible until after World War II.*

A   1821

B   1834

A *The Palace of Westminster in 1821.*

B *The fire on 16 October 1834.*

C *After the fire, the walls of gutted buildings still stand.*

D *Sir Charles Barry's new Houses of Parliament.*

E & F *The eighteenth-century Law Courts.*

G *The demolished Law Courts revealing Westminster Hall.*

H *Painted false walls showing proposed restorations.*

I *Westminster Hall as restored after the removal of the Law Courts.*

C   1835

D   C1880

E   C1880

F   C1880

G   1883

H   1883

The Palace of Westminster

It was the principal residence of the kings of England until Henry VIII abandoned it in favour of Whitehall; thereafter it remained the administrative centre for the kingdom and the home of both Houses of Parliament. During the eighteenth century the medieval halls and chambers which made up the old Palace began to be surrounded by additional buildings until by the 1820s it was completely engulfed by the 'modern improvements' (**A**). The fire of 1834 (**B**) destroyed or gutted most of the Palace buildings and only Westminster Hall was completely saved.

Attached to the west side of Westminster Hall were the eighteenth-century Law Courts which mainly survived the fire and remained until 1883 (**E** and **F**) when the building of the new Royal Courts of Justice in the Strand made them redundant. With their demolition, the ancient wall of Westminster Hall, complete with its original flying buttresses, could be seen for the first time in centuries (**G**). Controversy raged as to how it should be restored and to help the debate false painted walls were erected to show what the restoration would look like (**H**) and a modified version of the proposal was carried out (**I**).

I   C1900

Parliament Square

THE TWO JOINED PHOTOGRAPHS on the right **(A)** were taken in 1886 from the tower of St Margaret's Church. On the left is King Street which until the eighteenth century was the only highway which led to Whitehall. Its narrowness is better illustrated in the photograph below **(B)** which was taken just after the pub on the corner was built in 1889. So inconvenient was this entrance to Whitehall that in 1738 an Act of Parliament resulted in the purchase of all the property from King Street to the Thames and the creation of a new thoroughfare. This was Parliament Street. The huge building across the other end of King Street and blocking it off as a direct route to Whitehall is Gilbert Scott's Home Office built in 1874.

B   C1890   A

C   1860S

1886

All the houses between King Street on the left and Parliament Street on the right, seen here **(C)** in the 1860s, were swept away in 1898 to make way for the 'New Government Offices' **(D)** designed by J.M. Brydon and built between 1900 and 1907. At the same time Parliament Street was widened to the same width as Whitehall. The statue is of Lord Derby, erected here in 1874 but since moved to the other side of the square.

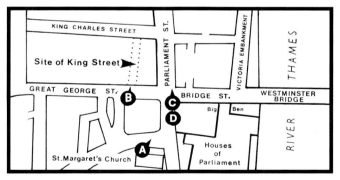

A *Looking across Parliament Square from the tower of St Margaret's Church in 1886. The statue is that of Peel.*

B *King Street in about 1890.*

C *Parliament Square in the 1860s with King Street on the left and Parliament Street on the right.*

D *The 'New Government Offices' built in 1907 completely obliterating King Street.*

D   **C1907**

A 1806

B 1860S

Westminster Abbey Precincts

THE TWO VIEWS ABOVE (**A** and **C**) have much in common; only the houses encroaching on the left are unfamiliar. Those nearest to us were demolished twenty years after the drawing was made to make way for Westminster Hospital (**D**). The single-storey building half-way down led to Westminster Market which was replaced by the Sessions House seen in (**D**) and (**E**). The elm trees in the churchyard were planted immediately after the coronation of George III and were cut down to make way for the scaffolding put up for spectators at the coronation of George IV.

The north transept of the Abbey is seen here (**B**) before Gilbert Scott restored it during the 1870s. But even this façade is not original; it had already been restored in the eighteenth century. The photograph was taken from the roof of the Sessions House, the pediment of which sticks out on the right.

In front of the west door of the Abbey the scholars of Westminster School put up a monument to their fellows who died in the Crimean War and the photograph (**D**) was taken just after it had been erected in 1861. Behind it is Westminster Hospital (1834) part of which, slightly altered, is on the left of (**C**). It was demolished in 1951. Next to it is the Sessions House (**E**) which was replaced by Middlesex Guildhall in 1913.

C

8612. WESTMINSTER ABBEY, (WEST

C1910

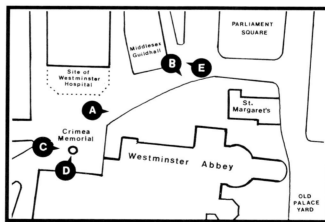

D 1860S E 1828

A *A water-colour by William Capon painted in 1823 from a drawing he made in October 1806.*

B *The north transept of Westminster Abbey sometime in the 1860s before Gilbert Scott's restorations, with St Margaret's Church on the left and the new Victoria Tower in the distance.*

C *A hardly-changed familiar view in about 1910.*

D *The Crimea Memorial with Westminster Hospital and the Sessions House.*

E *Westminster Guildhall or Sessions House.*

A

C1865

A *Old houses demolished to make way for the Royal Aquarium.*

B *The Royal Aquarium itself.*

C & D *Gilbert Scott's Westminster Chambers.*

E *The Crimea Memorial with Westminster Palace Hotel on the right.*

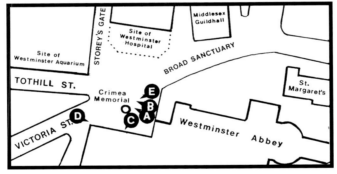

Broad Sanctuary

BROAD SANCTUARY, the ancient open space north of Westminster Abbey, was transformed in the 1860s and 70s. Some of the old houses which bordered it on the corner of Prince's Street and Tothill Street are pictured here **(A)** in about 1865. The railings around the Crimea Memorial can just be seen on the left. On the site of these houses was built one of London's most extraordinary places of entertainment, The Royal Aquarium **(B)**. Covering

C

1854 D

1860S

B   Z 25 ROYAL AQUARIUM, WESTMINSTER.   **C1876**

some two and a half acres with a 600-foot (182-metre) frontage along Tothill Street, it opened on 22 January 1876. With walls of Portland stone and a cast-iron and glass roof reminiscent of the Crystal Palace which inspired it, the building cost over £200,000. It had some thirty fish tanks, one of which was claimed to be the largest in the world, but they were seldom full of fish and it never caught on as an aquarium. And although its avowed aim was to provide 'intellectual enjoyment and educational advantage', it was never taken seriously and soon degenerated into a glorified music hall and side-show with freaks and sensational turns, like the pretty Zazel being fired from a cannon and scantily clad female swimmers performing aquatic feats in the great tank. It was demolished in 1903 and on its site was built the Wesleyan Central Hall, opened in 1912 as 'the Mecca of Methodism', and still standing. The still prominent memorial to the 'Old Westminsters' who died in the Crimea War (**E**) was designed by Gilbert Scott and erected in 1861. On its right is Westminster Palace Hotel, also finished in 1861. With 400 rooms, it was one of the earliest of London's luxury hotels and the first to install lifts. On the opposite corner is Westminster Chambers (**C** and **D**). Used now mainly as offices, but when it opened in 1854 this was a block of residential flats consisting of 120 self-contained suites of rooms. The oriel window on the corner (**D**) was, according to a contemporary writer, 'a novelty in English street architecture'.

E   **1860S**

Whitehall 1

WITH THE DEMOLITION OF KING STREET (see p. 72), Parliament Street was considerably widened but not enough, to judge by this photograph **(A)**, published in 1901, to prevent a bottleneck worthy of a modern traffic jam. Parliament Street was created in the eighteenth century and some of the houses on the left date from this time. Just behind the trees is the end of Richmond Terrace which was recently restored. Where Parliament Street becomes Whitehall **(B)**, the first turning on the left is Downing Street, with Gilbert Scott's Home Office of 1874 on the nearer corner and the New Treasury Offices remodelled by Charles Barry in 1846 on the other corner.

Downing Street was originally a cul-de-sac with plain brick houses on three sides **(D)**. The south side was replaced by the Home Office in 1874 and the end houses demolished in 1876 to make the opening into St James's Park **(E)**. Of the original houses only Nos. 10, 11 and 12 remain.

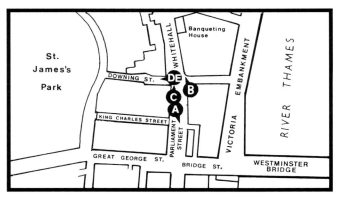

A   1901

B   1899

C   1880S

A *Congestion in Parliament Street in 1901.*

B *Treasury Building in 1899.*

C *Whitehall with the Banqueting House in the centre the only visible remains of the old Palace of Whitehall. On the right is the entrance to Richmond Terrace.*

D *Downing Street was originally built as a cul-de-sac as seen here in 1846.*

E *The opening into St James's Park was made in 1876. No. 10 is the house nearest the camera.*

D   1846

E   C1880

A   1884

B   C1909

C   C1919

Horse Guards at Whitehall, London

D   C1901

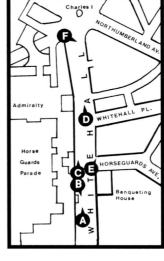

A *Whitehall looking north in 1884 and* **B** *looking in the opposite direction, with the portico of Dover House appearing in both photographs.*

C *This photograph of Horse-guards could almost have been taken today.*

D *The Admiralty.*

E *The old War Office, new in 1906.*

F *The tall Victorian building still stands where Whitehall joins Charing Cross.*

E   C1910

Whitehall 2

THE OLD PALACE OF WHITEHALL once covered 24 acres; the only building still standing is Inigo Jones's Banqueting House of 1622 seen on the right (A). The narrow turning beyond it is Whitehall Yard. On the other corner is a handsome mansion called Carrington House designed by Sir William Chambers and built in 1764. When Whitehall Yard was widened to make the modern Horseguards Avenue it was proposed that Carrington House be moved northward on rollers but the cost prohibited the idea and the house was demolished in 1886. On the left is Dover House built in 1758. Its portico, facing the street, also seen on the right of (B), was added in 1788. Horseguards (C) and the Admiralty (D) remain much the same today as when they were built. The modernization of the east side of Whitehall began when the War Office was built between 1899 and 1906 (E) on the site of Carrington House. It contained 1,000 rooms and about 2½ miles of corridors.

This photograph by William Strudwick (F) was taken just after the central building was erected in 1865. Miraculously it still stands today though everything around it has been rebuilt long ago. The privately owned telegraph station would be taken over by the Post Office in the government's nationalization of 1869. The firm of Stanford, the map makers, still exists but their premises are now in Long Acre.

F   C1865

A   1850

Trafalgar Square

THE ONE THING all the pictures on this page have in common is the equestrian statue of Charles I which has been in the same position, looking down Whitehall, ever since it was put there in 1676. In those days Charing Cross was a very different place (**B**). To the north was the King's Mews with its great open stable yard boxed in by shabby buildings which included the rambling Golden Cross coaching inn, and where the Strand began, stood the huge Jacobean town house of the Dukes of Northumberland. By 1830, apart from the modernizing of the Golden Cross, little else had changed (**C**) but immediately afterwards this whole block was to be demolished leaving an open space ready to become Trafalgar Square. Now St Martin-in-the-Fields could be seen with Morley's Hotel in front of it (**D**). Nelson on his column was put up in 1843 but twenty-four years were to pass before Landseer's lions arrived despite their appearance in the engraving of 1850 (**A**). The National Gallery now stands on the site of the King's Mews buildings. With the demolition of Northumberland House in 1875 (**E**) and the formation of Northumberland Avenue (**F**), the Square finally took on its familiar appearance.

The map shows eighteenth-century Charing Cross superimposed in grey on the modern map.

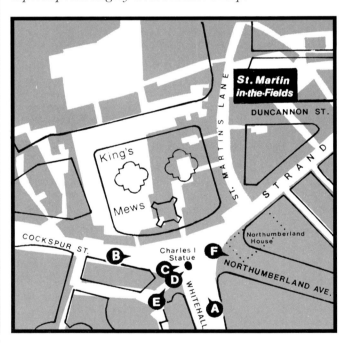

B   1740

C   1830

D   1842

E   **C1890**

F   **C1890**

A *Though engraved in 1850 this view shows Trafalgar Square almost exactly as it is today. The lions had to be imagined.*

B *Charing Cross in 1740 showing the King's Mews on the left with Charles I's statue and Northumberland House in the background.*

C *Little here has changed since the last view was drawn ninety years before.*

D *The Golden Cross and its neighbouring houses have been swept away for the creation of Trafalgar Square.*

E *Trafalgar Square assumes its present form.*

F *Looking down Northumberland Avenue.*

A 1828

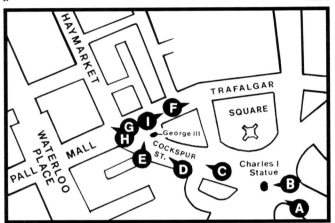

B C1870

C 1827

D 1880S

Cockspur Street

THE SLUMS WHICH CLUTTERED the vicinity of Charles I's statue in the eighteenth century were swept away during the course of the 1820s to make way for the grand Metropolitan Improvements inspired by John Nash.

The large building behind the Charles I statue (**A** and **B**) was designed by Smirke to house the Royal College of Physicians and the Union Club whose façade (**C**) was remodelled in 1925 when it became Canada House.

All that remains today in this photo (**D**) is the equestrian statue of George III put up in 1836. On the west corner of the Haymarket is the Italian Opera House or Her Majesty's Theatre seen more clearly in photo (**G**). This theatre, the second on the site, was built in 1790 but the exterior, including the colonnades, was added in 1818. In 1892 the theatre was demolished and on the site was built the huge French Renaissance-style block (**H**), only the northern part of which contained the new, and still standing, Theatre. The other two-thirds was occupied by the Carlton Hotel until 1957 when it was pulled down to make way for New Zealand House.

The central building (**E**) was the United Universities Club demolished in 1902; on the right is Waterloo House built originally as a glass manufacturer's show room. (**F**) The creation of Pall Mall East in the 1820s opened up the view to St Martin-in-the-Fields and the King's Mews on the left which was replaced by the National Gallery in 1838 (**I**). The still-existing portico belongs to the Royal College of Physicians.

E   1827

F   C1827

A & B *The Charles I statue, still on the same site today.*

C & D *The fifty-odd years which separate these two views along Cockspur Street show little change.*

E *This island site is now occupied by George III's statue.*

F & I *Pall Mall East.*

G *Her Majesty's Theatre with its colonnade which was added in 1818.*

H *The Carlton Hotel with Her Majesty's behind it.*

G   1870S

H   C1899

I   C1900

A C1900

A *Pall Mall crossing Waterloo Place with the Guards' Memorial on the left.*

B *Looking up Regent Street soon after it had been built.*

C *Waterloo Place with the Athenaeum on the left and*

the United Services Club on the right.

D *Looking towards Piccadilly Circus.*

E *Charles II Street with the Junior United Services Club on the corner.*

F *The club as rebuilt in 1857 with the Theatre Royal Haymarket in the distance.*

B 1828

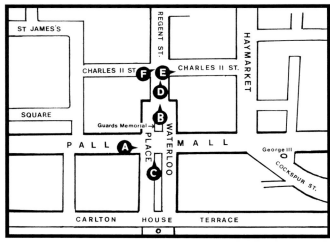

C 1910

D   1880

Around Waterloo Place

Nash designed Waterloo Place as a grand formal square fronting the Prince Regent's Carlton House with a splendid vista up Regent Street to Piccadilly Circus (B). In 1860 the Guards' Memorial, commemorating the 2,162 members of the Brigade of Guards who died in the Crimea War, was put up (A). It was moved 26 feet (11 metres) back in 1914 to make room for the statues of Florence Nightingale and Lord Herbert. Nash planned two clubhouses for either side of Waterloo Place, both of which still stand (C). On the right, also seen in (A), is the United Services which Nash designed himself and on the left is the Athenaeum by Decimus Burton and erected in 1830. The equestrian statue is of Lord Robert Napier, unveiled in 1891 and moved to Queen's Gate in 1921 to make way for the national memorial to Edward VII.

Many of the buildings here (D) are survivors of Nash's original plan, as can be seen by comparison with the print (B). Nash had a happy knack of terminating his vistas with some eye-catching feature; here it is the old County Fire Office in Piccadilly Circus. The most prominent intrusion is the Junior United Services Club built in 1857 (F). It replaced the original clubhouse seen on the left of (E) designed by Smirke and dating from 1819. Then, as now, the Theatre Royal Haymarket ends the vista looking down Charles II Street and on the right is the northern colonnade of the Italian Opera House.

E   1827

F   1880s

A   C1843

B   1812

Clubland

The great clubhouses have given Pall Mall the nickname, 'The Street of Palaces'. We have already seen the United Services and the Athenaeum on the corners of Waterloo Place (A). Next to the Athenaeum are the Travellers (1832) and the Reform (1841), both by Barry. The next club, after the gap of Carlton Gardens, is the Carlton seen in (C) in its original form as built by Robert Smirke in 1836 and as rebuilt in 1856 on the right of (D). It was destroyed by a bomb in 1940.

In St James's Square (B) many of the houses on the left still stand and the church of St James's Piccadilly rises above them.

The last club was the extraordinary Junior Naval and Military (E) opened in 1875. As it overlooked the grounds of Marlborough House its architect was not allowed to put any windows at the back or side. That left only the Pall Mall front to admit light and since that faced north the sun never entered it. 'The Club in which the sun never shines' lasted only three years. The building, however, was not demolished until 1930.

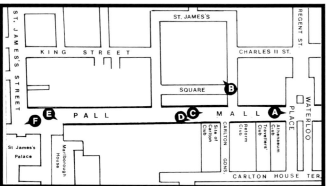

C   1842

D   **C1896**

A *Where Pall Mall's Clubland begins.*

B *St James's Square before the trees hid the statue of William III from view.*

C *The Carlton, Reform, Travellers, Athenaeum and United Services Clubs.*

D *In the 1890s the north side of Pall Mall had far fewer clubs but some eighteenth-century houses surviving.*

E *Junior Naval and Military Club with Marlborough House in the background.*

F *This view of St James's Palace has hardly changed.*

E   **1878**

F   **1819**

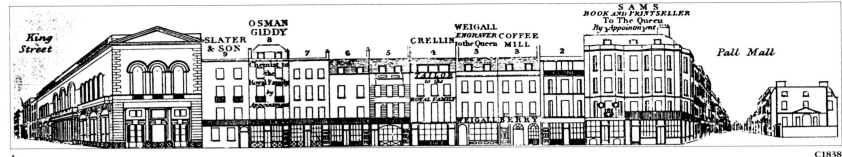

A   C1838

St James's Street

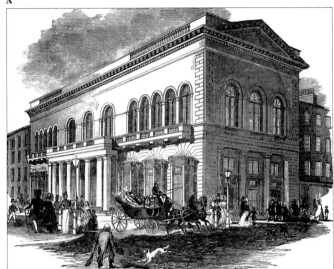

C   1844

D   1926

THE SOUTHERN END of St James's Street boasts two of the most perfect eighteenth-century shop-fronts in London numbered 3 and 6 in Tallis's street view above **(A)**. The pair of houses at No. 3 on the right of photograph **(B)** were built in the early 1700s and their shop-fronts date from the late eighteenth century. Originally a grocer's, hence the sign of the Coffee Mill, it has been a wine merchant's since the Berry family took it over in 1812. By the side of the shop is the passage leading to Pickering Place **(D)**; dating from the 1730s and once notorious for its gambling hells, it is hardly changed today. No. 6, three doors up, has been occupied by Locks, the hatters, since 1765 and the building is even earlier. Here Nelson and Wellington bought their hats. St James's Bazaar **(C)** was built in 1832 for William Crockford, the owner of the famous St James's Street gaming club, as a shopping centre but it failed after only a year. Thereafter it became residential chambers, an exhibition hall and a clubhouse. It was altered in 1881 to its appearance in the photograph and again in 1914.

A *Elevation of St James's Street from Tallis's Street Views about 1838.*

B *The east side in the 1890s still has all the buildings seen in Tallis except one.*

C *St James's Bazaar in 1844 when it was exhibiting proposed designs for the decoration of the New Houses of Parliament.*

D *Pickering Place. The photograph, taken in 1926, could have been taken at any time since it was built in the 1730s so little has it changed. It was here according to legend, that the last duel in London was fought.*

B   C1890

TRAFALGAR SQUARE
TO ST PAUL'S

ABOVE *A view of Ludgate Circus from the top of a bus in the 1890s.*

THE ONE-TIME slums of Charing Cross were transformed into this great open space 160 years ago and age has not diminished its grandeur. There are still splendid buildings all around and, from where we start our walk, the view down Whitehall to Big Ben is one of the sights of London.

James Gibbs's church of St Martin-in-the-Fields was not seen as we see it today until the slums which hid it from view were demolished in the 1820s. Its beautiful design, unique at the time, became the inspiration for churches throughout America.

The Strand still has that sense of fun which all its theatres and restaurants conferred upon it a hundred years ago. Not for nothing was its most famous theatre called The Gaiety. It ends abruptly after Aldwych where the monumental Victorian Law Courts, more Gothic than any genuine Gothic buildings ever were, prepare us for the sobriety of Fleet Street. For this is a particularly sad spot today with all its newspaper printers gone and nothing to replace them.

And Ludgate Circus has changed too, literally out of all recognition. The old King Lud pub hangs on to the front of a new building by the skin of its teeth, but all else has changed, and changed for the worse as we approach St Paul's. So banal are the new erections here that we even miss the ugly old railway viaduct which caused such an outcry when it was first put up. It is a welcome relief when, half-way up the hill, Wren takes over and gives us the spindly spire of St Martin Ludgate as a foil to the mighty dome of St Paul's. With buildings sticking out on the left, the full frontal view of St Paul's is not achieved until you are quite close to it. Then it is as overwhelming as ever it was and the views from the south, where pre-war buildings were destroyed in the blitz, are now more open than they ever were in the past.

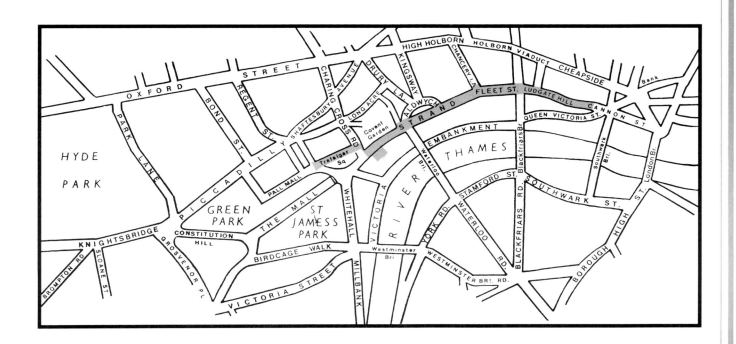

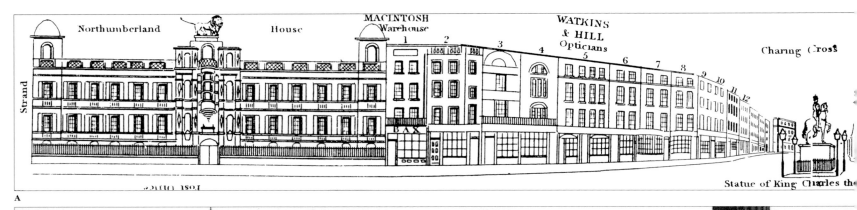

A

B

C

C1874

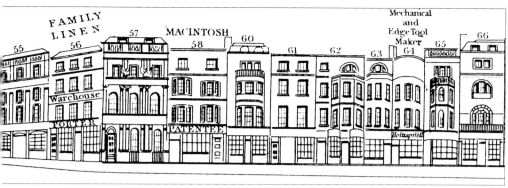

C1839

Trafalgar Square

THE LAST TIME we saw Trafalgar Square we approached it from Whitehall; here we are looking south from the National Gallery. Tallis's view (A) was drawn in about 1839 after the slums around the King's Mews had been cleared away ready for the creation of the Square. Most of his houses and shops were still standing 30 years later and are easily recognizable in the photo (B). Two new buildings have appeared; one on the right and the tall one to the left of Nelson's Column which appears in detail on page 81. Prominent on the left of both pictures is Northumberland House, the great Jacobean town house of the Dukes of Northumberland. This was demolished in 1874 to make way for Northumberland Avenue and its ruins can be seen in (C) and (D).

Occupying the whole eastern side of Trafalgar Square was Morley's Hotel (C). Built in 1831 with 100 rooms, it was the largest and most handsome of London's early hotels, but in 1921 it was acquired by the South African government and rebuilt as South Africa House. King George V opened it in 1933. Behind it on this new island site was a recreated Golden Cross Hotel.

The equestrian statue (C) is of George IV by Chantry. It was designed to stand on top of Marble Arch but by the time it was finished the idea was abandoned and it was put here temporarily while a permanent site was found. That was in 1843 and it has been there ever since.

C1869

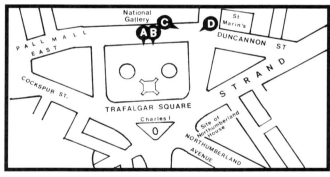

A *Tallis's elevation of the south side of Trafalgar Square.*

B *The same view after Nelson's Column had been erected.*

C *Morley's Hotel and the statue of George IV.*

D *West side of the Square.*

D

1874

A   1794

B   1792

A, B & C Three late eighteenth-century views of St Martin-in-the-Fields: A from the King's Mews, B from St Martin's Lane and C from the unnamed thoroughfare on the north of the church still existing today, with St Martin's Lane in the background.

D St Martin's Place, drawn in 1886. 'The Theatre' is an advertisement for the periodical of that name.

E The statue of General Gordon standing temporarily where Nurse Cavell's memorial was later erected.

St Martin's Place

UNTIL THE LATE 1820s, the view of St Martin-in-the-Fields was obscured by a clutter of mean houses facing the King's Mews and backing on to St Martin's Lane (**A**). On the south side was the church's burial ground (**B**), removed to make way for Duncannon Street. When all the houses in front of the church were demolished, St Martin's Place was created (**D**). In this drawing of 1886 the building on the right is recognizable still standing on the corner of St Martin's Lane. Just behind it a year later, Charing Cross Road was opened and in 1896 the scene changed again when the National Portrait Gallery was built. It can be seen behind the bus in photo (**E**) with Charing Cross Road in the background. Less familiar is General Gordon on his camel. This was erected here temporarily in 1902 before being shipped off to Khartoum. Standing on the site today is the memorial to Nurse Edith Cavell.

C   1795

D   1886

E   1902

A

Charing Cross Station

THIS PART OF THE STRAND up to Villiers Street has changed remarkably little (**A**). The circular building on the left is one of the famous 'pepper-pot' corners of Nash's triangular block which he built in 1830–32. Charing Cross Station, the West End terminus of the Southern Railway, was ready for business in January 1864 and the 250-bedroom Hotel on its Strand frontage was opened on 15 May the following year. It was designed by E.M. Barry who was also responsible for the reconstruction of the Eleanor Cross in the forecourt. The Hotel was badly damaged in the war, and it was not until 1951 that it was completely restored with its original roof, 'borrowed from the Louvre in Paris', being replaced by a new top storey. Plans for widening the Strand here had been discussed since the turn of the century but it was only in 1958 that the old railings of the station forecourt were removed and the two gateway lodges demolished. Originally these had been miniature police stations but were later rented, the far one to a tobacconist, the other to Hands & Co. who ran a *bureau de change* for the considerable European trade … six Continental services a day … London to Paris in eight hours. Today the iron railings and stone pillars are back, copies of the old ones, complete with reproductions of the globular lamps seen in photo (**B**).

A *The beginning of the Strand at Charing Cross, at the turn of the century.*

B *The Eleanor Cross in the station forecourt dates from only 1865. The original, the last of twelve erected by* Edward I to mark where the body of his Queen Eleanor rested on its way to burial in Westminster Abbey, had stood at the top of Whitehall where Charles I now stands.

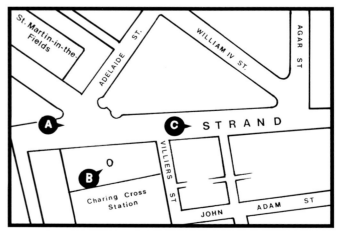

B **C1880**

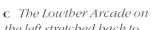

C1900

C The Lowther Arcade on the left stretched back to Adelaide Street and was famous for its fancy shops and toy bazaars. It was destroyed in 1902 when Coutts' Bank was built here. This has since been replaced by a glass wall totally ruining Nash's Regency façade. The corner building beyond Nash's block was designed for an insurance company by C.R. Cockerell in 1831 and was demolished in 1908. The British Medical Association building, complete with Epstein sculptures, replaced it and still stands.

C **C1890**

A   1880S

A *Congestion in the western end of the Strand before it was widened.*

B *John Street, Adelphi (now John Adam Street) in 1795 showing the Society of Arts on the left.*

C *Adam Street, Adelphi with a glimpse of the Strand in the background.*

D *Seventeenth-century buildings next door to the Adelphi Theatre.*

E *A contrast in architectural styles on the corner of Adam Street and the Strand.*

F *A widened, Edwardian Strand, with the Savoy buildings on the right.*

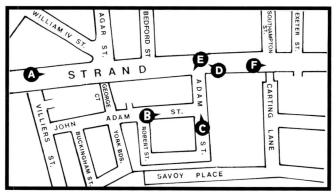

The Strand

THE NECESSITY FOR WIDENING the Strand is clearly demonstrated in this congested view (A) just east of Villiers Street. Any turning on the right would lead to the peace and quiet of the Adelphi, that impressive development of terrace houses built by the Adam Brothers in the 1770s. Their great block of residential chambers which fronted the Thames (see pp. 124–5) was demolished in 1936 but some of the individual buildings still stand, elegant reminders of what has been lost to us. Most notable

B   1795   **C**   1796

is the headquarters of the Society of Arts (**B**), unchanged today, and in Adam Street (**C**) more original buildings are recognizable. No. 7, facing us at the end of the street in (**B**), is one of the best examples still standing. The handsome classical block on the corner of Adam Street continues round into the Strand where the photograph (**E**) shows it rubbing shoulders with a wonderfully flamboyant mid-Victorian shop, illustrating a typical contrast which made the Strand such an interesting mixture of architectural styles and periods. Some of the Strand's buildings which survived well into the twentieth century went back at least as far as the 1600s. Two such buildings, with their typical projecting bays, stood next door to the Adelphi Theatre (**D**) while a similar one can be glimpsed facing the entrance to Adam Street in (**C**).

When its south side was widened at the turn of the century, the Strand lost nothing of architectural value but gained the imposing new entrance to the Savoy Hotel (**F**). Before these twin blocks were erected in 1904, the Savoy's entrance had been on the Thames side of the building.

The bill-posted block, jutting out on the right (**F**), contained Terry's Theatre. This was built in 1887, became a cinema in 1910 and was finally demolished in 1923.

D   1904

E   1883

F   1905

A 1897

B 1905

'Let's All Go Down The Strand'

THE OLD MUSIC-HALL SONG captures the spirit of the Victorian Strand as a place of 'fun and joys' with no fewer than eleven theatres at the turn of the century. Most famous of all was the Gaiety, home of musical comedy, burlesque and comic opera, destined to be forever remembered for its Gaiety Girls and stage-door Johnnies. The original theatre, which opened in 1868, had a most unprepossessing entrance on the Strand seen here **(A)** in 1897. It was, however, the first theatre frontage to be lit by electricity, and had been since 1 August 1878. The white glass globes of the electric lamps can be seen over the awning and outside Spiers & Pond's Gaiety Restaurant. A new Gaiety Theatre was already in the course of construction when the old theatre was closed on 4 July 1903 to make way for the creation of Aldwych. The new Gaiety **(B)**, with its impressive baroque facade designed by the great Norman Shaw, was opened on 26 October 1903. The relationship between the old and the new Gaietys can be seen by comparing the two photographs. The offices of the *Morning Post* to the left of the old Gaiety entrance in **(A)** and on the left in **(B)** are the same building. In 1906 the *Morning Post* offices were demolished, as can be seen in **(C)**, and rebuilt a little further back **(D)**. **(C)** also shows some still-existing buildings on the left with Henekey's about to open. The new Gaiety Theatre was closed in 1939 and demolished in 1957.

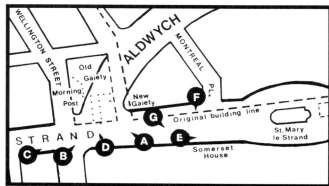

C 1906

D 1906

E   1896

The Strand Before Aldwych

THE CREATION OF ALDWYCH destroyed everything to the north of St Mary-le-Strand Church
(E). On the left of the church is the entrance to
Holywell Street no wider than a lane (see p. 102)
and behind it are houses standing on the north side of
the Strand creating a narrow bottleneck approach to
the City.

The south side, however, was unaffected by the
new improvements and many old buildings still
stand on either side of Somerset House. Those on
the west side (G) are recognizable today and are virtually the same buildings which appeared in Tallis's
Street Views in 1838 (F). None of the firms doing
business in 1838 was present in 1901, when the
photograph was taken, and today all the shop fronts
have been altered.

F   1838

A *Entrance to the old
Gaiety Theatre.*

B *The new Gaiety with the
rest of Aldwych still in the
course of building.*

C *The old premises of the
Morning Post almost
demolished.*

D *This iron skeleton looks
deceptively like the new
Gaiety being built. It is,
however, the new Morning
Post offices which are being
constructed on their old site
but a little further back. The
finished building still exists.*

E *All the buildings on the
left were demolished to
create Aldwych. Those on
the right remain today.*

F *Tallis's elevation of 1838
showing buildings still
standing today although
their shops have been
altered.*

G *The same buildings
photographed in 1901.*

G   1901

A   1876

B   1898

D   1910

The Making of Aldwych

THE AREA ON THE NORTH SIDE of the church of St Mary-le-Strand that was cleared for the building of Aldwych was a maze of ancient lanes and alleys and narrow streets. The two most important were Wych Street (A) and Holywell Street (B), sometimes called Booksellers' Row, infamous for the shops selling indecent books and obscene prints. Both these thoroughfares were narrow and lined with picturesque old houses dating back to Tudor and Stuart times and their destruction was greatly lamented by antiquarians. In both views, the steeple of St Clement Danes can be seen in the background. As the old map shows and as we can see in the photograph (C), the houses on the north side of the Strand came down level with the south side of the church of St Mary and made the thoroughfare extremely narrow. The glass canopy under the bill-boards leads to the Opera Comique, a theatre actually between Wych Street and Holywell Street which had to be reached via a long tunnel from this entrance in the Strand. In the distance is the steeple of St Clement Danes and the towers of the Law Courts.

The clearing of the twenty-eight acres needed for the creation of the Aldwych crescent began in the 1890s and opened up a vast empty area north of St Mary-le-Strand (D). One of the first buildings to arrive on the empty site was Victoria House seen here (E) in splendid isolation. It was built in 1908 by the government of Victoria but when the Australian government took over this eastern corner of Aldwych they incorporated this building into their palatial Australia House. Although its upper storey has been altered, this corner is still recognizable. This photo was taken in 1913, the same year that King George V laid the foundation stone of Australia House. Due to delays caused by the war it was not opened until 1918.

The Underground station on the right was called The Strand when it opened in 1907. It was renamed Aldwych in 1915 and is still open during rush hours.

A *Wych Street in 1876.*

B *Holywell Street or Booksellers' Row just before demolition.*

C *The narrow eastern end of the Strand before the buildings on the north side were demolished.*

D *St Mary-le-Strand, 1910.*

E *Victoria House, one of the first of the Aldwych buildings.*

C

C1889

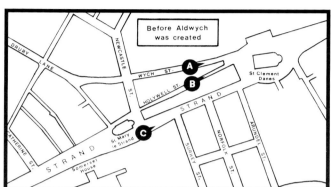

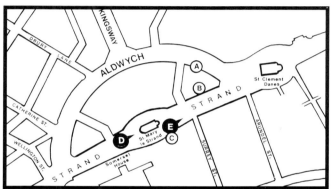

E

1913

A   C1900

A *The church of St Clement Danes rebuilt by Wren with a steeple added in 1819.*

B *The Strand south of the church with the United Kingdom Provident Institution on the corner of Milford Lane.*

C *The building on the left became a pub, The George, in 1891 and was given its 'Tudor' front in the 1930s.*

D *This view vanished completely when Aldwych was created. On the left is Holywell Street, on the right Wych Street.*

Around St Clement Danes

THE CHURCH OF ST CLEMENT DANES (A) has always stood on an island site. In the early days its north side was only a few feet away from a row of slum properties which was swept away in the 1790s and replaced by a bright new crescent called Pickett Place. But the whole area surrounding the church was completely changed with the building of the Law Courts in 1874 and Aldwych in 1905. The creation of Aldwych destroyed two narrow streets called Wych Street and Holywell Street (see p. 102) the eastern ends of which can be seen in (D). The pub, the Rising Sun, and the bookshop next to it can also be seen on the right of (C). The changes south of the church were not so drastic. The crescent of mainly Georgian houses and shops received its first 'modern' intrusion in 1902 when the United Kingdom Provident Institution built their grand baroque headquarters on the corner of Milford Lane (B). It was destroyed in the 1970s.

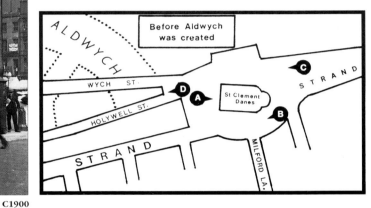

B   C1907

C   C1890

D   C1900

Temple Bar

TEMPLE BAR WAS LITERALLY, and is now by name only, the gateway to the City from Westminster, the spot where even the monarch must acknowledge the City's unique and exclusive position in London's government. Originally a bar or barrier, the famous gate was erected in 1670 but there is no documentary evidence to support the belief that it was designed by Sir Christopher Wren. The view from the Strand drawn by Shotter Boys in 1842 (A) shows not only the unmistakable tower of St Dunstan-in-the-West, but a more humble building which can still be seen today. Clearly numbered 229, it dates from before the Great Fire and is now occupied by the Wig & Pen Club. It is seen again in (D and E) together with its equally ancient neighbour which also still stands.

Another survival of the old Strand is the entrance to Twinings the Tea Merchants, seen squeezed between two great blocks in (F). It has been here since 1787.

Both sides of Temple Bar were identical except for the statues in the niches. On the Strand side, also seen in (B), were the figures of Charles I and Charles II; on the Fleet Street side (C) they were of Queen Elizabeth and James I. Beyond Temple Bar in (C) can be seen the back of St Clement Danes and, on the right, an open area cleared to make way for the Law Courts. Temple Bar was demolished in 1878 and re-erected in Theobald's Park, Hertfordshire, where it now languishes in spite of efforts to return it. In 1880 the present memorial (G) was erected on its site.

A   1842

B   C1865

C   C1871

D   1926

E   1921

F   1920S

Law Courts

BELL YARD

S T R A N D

St.
Clement
Danes

FLEET
ST.

Site of
Temple Bar

A & B *The Strand side of Temple Bar, drawn in 1842 and photographed about twenty years later.*

C *Temple Bar from Fleet Street with an open space cleared for the building of the Law Courts.*

D & E *Two pre-Fire houses*

still standing in the Strand.

F *The eighteenth-century entrance to Twinings.*

G *The Griffin (actually a dragon) Memorial which replaced Temple Bar in 1880.*

G   C1907

107

Old Buildings near ye Temple Gate in Fleet...

A   18TH CENTURY

The WAX WORK

B   1807

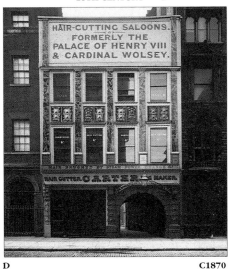

C   1838

HAIR-CUTTING SALOONS.
FORMERLY THE
PALACE OF HENRY VIII
& CARDINAL WOLSEY.

D   C1870

Prince Henry's Room

THE TENEMENT OVER THE STONE GATEWAY to Inner Temple was built in 1611 replacing an inn called the Prince's Arms. What happened to its Fleet Street frontage over the centuries is illustrated on this page. (A) shows what must have been its original state; (B) when it was Mrs Salmon's Waxworks; (C) in 1838 when the roof gables were boarded up and it became a hairdressers. It continued as a hair-cutting saloon (D and E) ('formerley the Palace of Henry VIII') until 1898 when it was bought by the LCC to prevent its demolition and carefully restored to the condition we see it in today.

E   1885

F   1906

St Dunstan-in-the-West

THE ORIGINAL CHURCH of St Dunstan-in-the-West projected some 30 feet (9 metres) out into Fleet Street (**G**) and in order to widen the thoroughfare it was demolished in 1829. Part of the old building was allowed to remain as a sort of screen behind which the new church was built (**H**) much further back. It was consecrated on 31 July 1833 and Fleet Street widened and straightened. Some of the features of the old church still survive. Its famous bracket clock of 1671 projecting over the street (**G**) with its giants striking the hours with clubs went first to a house in Regent's Park but was brought back to the new church by Lord Rothermere in 1935. The statue of Queen Elizabeth in her niche (**G**), originally over old Ludgate, also stands by the side of the church today.

Common to all these pictures are the two Elizabethan houses with balconies and pointed gables. They just escaped the Great Fire of 1666 that destroyed the whole of Fleet Street and died out almost at their doors. They survived until 1893.

G   1800

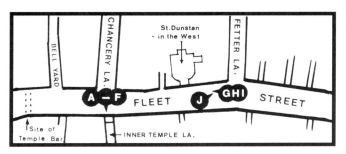

H   1832

I   1893

J   C1892

A–F *The south side of Fleet Street at various periods showing the tenement over the stone gateway to the Inner Temple.*

G *North side of Fleet Street with Temple Bar in the distance.*

H *The new church of St Dunstan-in-the-West behind the ruins of the old church.*

I *St Dunstan's before the bracket clock was replaced.*

J *Old houses which survived the Great Fire.*

A   1883

East End of Fleet Street

T HE NARROWNESS OF FLEET STREET is clearly
seen in the photo above (A) and in 1897 a programme of widening the street to a uniform 60 feet
(18 metres) began. It took twenty years to complete
and necessitated the demolition and gradual
rebuilding of the entire south side. The building line
of the north side, however, was not altered, but
many old houses were replaced by imposing newspaper offices like the original *Daily Telegraph*
building (B).

In 1931, only a few years after the photo (C) was
taken, this corner of Shoe Lane was transformed
when the sensationally modern *Daily Express* building, all black glass and chromium, arose on this site.
By contrast, almost opposite is Wren's lovely wed-
ding-cake spire of St Bride's Church here seen (D)
beautifully framed by the neo-classical houses and
shops designed by John Papworth and built in 1825
after a fire the year before.

B   1923

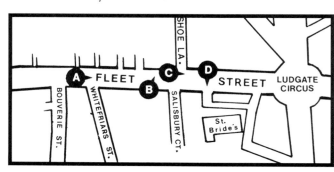

C   1920S

A   *Fleet Street in 1883 before its south side was widened.*

B   *The 1882* Daily Telegraph *building which was rebuilt in 1928.*

C   *Fleet Street in the late 1920s.*

D   *St Bride's Church viewed down St Bride's Avenue in about 1827.*

D   C1827

1890S

B   C1880

Ludgate Circus

THE PRESERVATION OF THE VIEW which Wren intended – the elegant spire of St Martin Ludgate acting as a foil against St Paul's swelling dome – prompted over a thousand people to sign a petition of protest when, in 1863, the news leaked out that the City Corporation was about to permit a railway viaduct to be built across the bottom of Ludgate Hill. The official ear was as deaf to such protests then as it is now and the viaduct was built in 1866. It carried the trains of the London Chatham and Dover Railway to link up with the Metropolitan Railway at Farringdon Street; the first time that trains had ever crossed the City from south of the river. The cast-iron viaduct, described by a contemporary as 'a miracle of clumsy and stubborn ugliness', was decorated with the City arms and proudly bore the insignia of the Railway on the brackets. It was replaced just before the last war and has now been demolished. Ludgate Hill suffered badly in the blitz but the King Lud public house managed to avoid destruction.

The photograph (A) shows two obelisks. The one on the right was erected in 1775 as a tribute to John Wilkes for his mayoralty and the one on the left commemorates another Lord Mayor, Robert Waithman, who died in 1833. Early in his life he had opened a linen-draper's shop at the southern end of Fleet Market, which ran down the middle of what was to become Farringdon Street, and the obelisk was erected on the site of his shop a few months after his death. In (B) we see the obelisk again and behind it is a triangular building dating from 1871 which still stands. Today Waithman's obelisk can be found in Salisbury Square.

A *Ludgate Circus was created in 1864 when the railway arrived. The façade of the King Lud public house has been incorporated into the present building on the site.*

B *The obelisk in memory of Lord Mayor Waithman. Behind it is St Bride's Street built between 1868 and 1871 as part of the Holborn Viaduct development.*

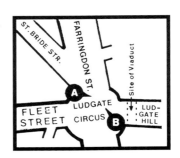

A   1812

New Bridge Street

WHEN NEW BRIDGE STREET was first built in 1764 by covering over the River Fleet it was merely an approach road to the new Blackfriars Bridge (A). But with the formation of Farringdon Street (B) and later Farringdon Road, the first direct route connecting south London with the north was created. Appropriately the first railway to cross the river into the City ran by its side. This was the London Chatham and Dover Railway which ended at Ludgate Hill Station. The forecourt approach to the station is on the right in photo (C). When it opened on 1 June 1865 it had all the importance of a main-line terminus bringing south London commuters into the heart of the City for the first time, but only seven months later the line was extended and it became a through station. As more stations opened, Ludgate Hill declined and in 1925 its forecourt was built over with shops. Four years later it closed down completely.

The building on the corner of Fleet Street flying the flag is the headquarters of Thomas Cook the travel agents which was specially built for them in 1873. At the time this photo was taken – the summer of 1884 – they were planning the transport of an expedition to relieve General Gordon. Opposite Cook's is the Congregational Memorial Hall occupying the site of the Fleet Prison. It is seen more closely in (B) just after it had been built in 1872. It was demolished in 1969.

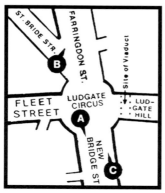

A *New Bridge Street before Ludgate Circus was created showing Wilkes's obelisk.*

B *The Congregational Memorial Hall is now demolished but the building on the left still stands.*

C *Holborn Viaduct in the distance beyond Ludgate Circus.*

B   C1872   C

1884

Ludgate to St Paul's

A   1842

WHEN THOMAS SHOTTER BOYS made this drawing in 1842 (**A**) Ludgate Hill was only 47 feet (14 metres) across and its widening between 1863 and 1891 resulted in the demolition of all the buildings on the right. Ludgate Hill at this time ended just before the church of St Martin's and then became Ludgate Street. The division marks the spot where Ludgate itself spanned the thoroughfare before it was demolished in 1762.

The Dean and Chapter of St Paul's jealously guarded the privacy of the Cathedral precincts and had insisted, to Wren's annoyance, that the west front should be enclosed by cast-iron railings. These can be seen in (**C**). Agitation for their removal began in 1834 but it was not until forty years later that the Chapter finally gave way and the railings were replaced by granite posts (**E**). At the same time the road on the south side (**G**) was considerably widened but the City's attempt to open the north side to vehicular traffic was vigorously opposed and the toll-gate (**B** and **D**) remained as a barrier until very recently.

The statue of Queen Anne surrounded by figures representing England, Ireland, North America and France (of which she was still notionally Queen) was made by Francis Bird and put up in 1712. She came in for some critical doggerel at the time. 'Brandy Nan, Brandy Nan, – You're left in the lurch, – With your face to the gin-shop, – And your back to the church.' Twice attacked by lunatics, she lost her sceptre, her orb, both arms and her nose, and in spite of being restored in 1883 the whole monument had fallen into decay by the time the photo (**F**) was taken. In 1884 it was removed and re-erected at Holmhurst, near St Leonards, Sussex, where it stands today. It was replaced by an exact copy in 1886.

A   *Ludgate Hill with the Old Bailey on the left.*

B & D   *The toll-gate in St Paul's churchyard is a reminder that traffic was always forbidden north of the Cathedral.*

C   *The Cathedral forecourt was enclosed by railings for over 160 years.*

E   *In 1874 the railings were removed and the forecourt opened to the public.*

F   *The original statue of Queen Anne in whose reign the Cathedral was finished.*

G   *The south side of St Paul's churchyard once had elegant shops and was wide enough for a cab-stand.*

B   1926

C   1798

D   1823

E

C1900

F

C1880

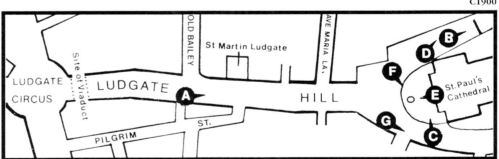

G

1823

St Paul's

ST PAUL'S CATHEDRAL (A), photographed from St Martin's Ludgate, dominated the skyline until well into the twentieth century. Whole areas around St Paul's were destroyed in the blitz opening up new views of the Cathedral that did not exist before the war. The incendiary bombs on the night of 29 December 1940, when St Paul's was ringed with fire, and the high explosives four months later, destroyed both sides of Cannon Street and most of Watling Street. All the Victorian buildings in (B) were destroyed, while in Watling Street (C) only the pillared building on the right and the one facing it across the road escaped the bombing.

A *St Paul's seen from the tower of St Martin's Ludgate.*

B *Cheapside about 1900 was narrower before the war-time destruction of* these Victorian office blocks.

C *The two foreground buildings are all that remain in the 1926 photograph.*

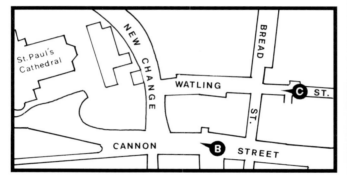

A   1890S

B   C1900

C   1926

THE EMBANKMENT TO LONDON BRIDGE

ABOVE *Early morning tranquillity on the Embankment.*

ACCEPTED TODAY as a normal part of the London scene, the Victoria Embankment is actually one of the great masterpieces of Victorian engineering. The roadway is merely a roofing-over of the Underground Railway and London's main sewer. Before it was built, all sewage ran straight into the Thames and the riverside was a picturesque, but unsavoury, jumble of wharves, warehouses and muddy foreshore.

There is a startling contrast in buildings soon after we begin our walk. The Victorian blocks erected when the Embankment was new give way to the extraordinary 'Post Modern' development which recently replaced the grimy Charing Cross Railway Station. Evidence of how far the Thames was pushed back to make way for the Embankment will be seen all along this walk, and the York Water Gate, high and dry in the gardens here, is a classic example. Somerset House was also once by the waterside and used to have boats moored against its walls.

Trams once rattled along the road here and the reclaimed land is green with trees and gardens. Statues of the famous and the forgotten abound and Cleopatra's Needle has been standing here for just a moment in its long history, for it was already old before London was thought of.

At Blackfriars we take the road which the Victorians built to connect the seat of government at Westminster with the seat of commerce in the City and arrive at London Bridge, where there has been a crossing of the Thames ever since the Romans founded London. Over the bridge we come to the spot where the railway first arrived in London. It brought to an end the great coaching age which is still remembered at our last stop, The George, London's sole surviving galleried coaching inn.

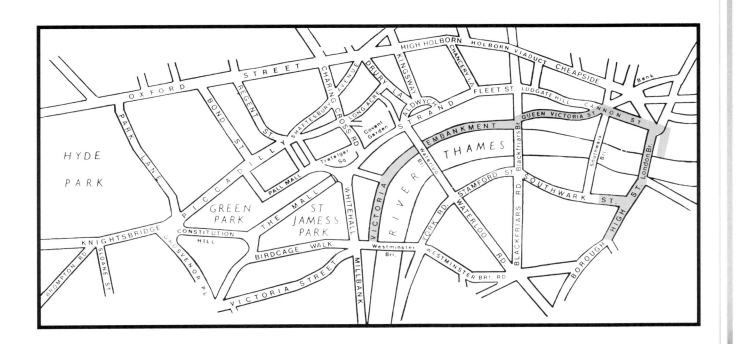

A   C1910

B   C1920

Victoria Embankment

THE VICTORIA EMBANKMENT was a remarkable engineering feat though in reality merely a covering over a sewer. Until it was built, London's sewage ran straight into the Thames. Sir Joseph Bazalgette devised a scheme by which all this sewage was fed into one great interceptor sewer, 8 feet (2.5 metres) in diameter, and carried over ten miles east to Barking. It was built along the foreshore of the Thames and roofed over to make a new roadway $1\frac{1}{3}$ miles (2 km) long and 100 feet (30m) wide. This was the Victoria Embankment, begun in 1864 and opened on 13 July 1870.

The landward side of the Embankment was at first cluttered with humble wharf-side houses which were only gradually replaced by new buildings. One of the first was the block built in 1874 to house St Stephen's Club (**C**). It still stands today and still incorporates the entrance to Westminster Underground Station.

The view in about 1880 (**E**) shows no new Embankment buildings but two old Whitehall mansions; on the left the back of the eighteenth-century Richmond Terrace and next to it Montagu House, built 1859-62 and now demolished. In the distance is the great mass of Charing Cross Station.

The first part of New Scotland Yard (**D**), finished in 1890, appears on the left of (**F**) together with the unmistakable pinnacles of Whitehall Court, shown more clearly in (**G**).

C   C1875

D   C1890

E   C1880

A *Trams rattle past New Scotland Yard and Boadicea's statue on their way to south London over Westminster Bridge.*

B *A familiar figure well into the 1920s was the bearded old gentleman who offered a penny a look at Big Ben through his telescope.*

C *St Stephen's Club with the entrance to Westminster Underground Station on its left.*

D *The first half of Norman Shaw's New Scotland Yard (1890).*

E *The Embankment before its houses were built with Charing Cross Station in the background.*

F *Heralding the great buildings yet to come, Whitehall Court dominates the skyline.*

G *The still-standing Whitehall Court with the statue of William Tyndale, erected in 1884, in the gardens.*

F   C1890

In 1907 Norman Shaw added his companion block to New Scotland Yard seen here **(A)** on the left. Although the LCC ran its first electric trams from Tooting to the foot of Westminster Bridge in 1903, it was not allowed to continue the line over the bridge for another three years. It was in December 1906 that electric trams first rattled past Queen Boadicea who had been driving her chariot since 1902.

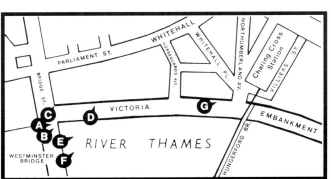

G   C1887

A C1888

B C1888

Northumberland Avenue

WHITEHALL COURT **(A)**, whose pinnacled and turreted skyline gives it the appearance of a fairy castle when seen from the other side of the river, is no more than a block of flats dating from 1884. Adjoining it on the corner is the National Liberal Club designed by Alfred Waterhouse. The club was founded by Gladstone as a metropolitan centre for country Liberals and it already had 6,000 members when it was opened in 1887.

The Hotel Metropole (1882-3) **(B)** with 700 rooms was one of the largest in London. Across the road is the Avenue Theatre built in 1882 by a speculator who believed that the adjoining railway would want to purchase the ground for an extension to Charing Cross Station. This never happened but ironically in 1905 part of the station collapsed on to the theatre, damaging it so badly that it had to be rebuilt. It reopened as The Playhouse in 1907.

Though Northumberland Avenue **(C)** was created in 1876 (see p. 93) its buildings did not start to go up until the 80s. The Constitutional Club of 1884 was one of the largest clubhouses in London.

The bridge which carries the South Eastern Railway over the Thames from Charing Cross Station **(D)** was begun in 1860, a few years before the Embankment was thought of. Had it already existed there is little doubt that Parliament would have insisted on something a little more decorative.

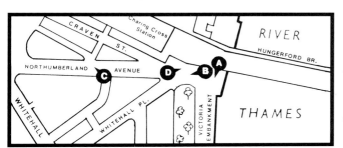

C   1880S

A *In the gardens in front of the National Liberal Club stands the statue of Sir James Outram, military commander in India. Erected in 1871, his was the first statue to be put up on the Embankment. Now there are thirteen.*

B *The cab rank complete with cabman's shelter is conveniently placed to serve the clubs and hotels of Northumberland Avenue. On the right is The Avenue Theatre, now the Playhouse.*

C *The Constitutional Club, Northumberland Avenue.*

D *Charing Cross Railway Bridge still carries trains to and from the southern counties as it has done for over 130 years.*

D   1890S

A   C1890

York Water Gate and the Adelphi

In the past the Strand was lined with great mansions belonging to the nobility whose gardens occupied the land gently sloping down to the Thames. (This slope is well illustrated in the Victorian photo of Villiers Street (A).) One of these great mansions was York House, now completely demolished except for its Water Gate (B), built in 1626 as a landing stage for boats (C) and now standing some 500 yards (457 metres) from the river showing how far the Embankment has been built out into the Thames. Also left high and dry by the building of the Embankment was the Adelphi, London's first block of flats, with its waterside terrace fronting on to the river (C). A wonderful example of town planning, it was built by the Adam Brothers in the 1770s on arches rising from the sloping river-bank. This unique architectural composition was destroyed in spite of enormous protests in 1936-8 leaving only a few fragments to remind us of what was lost (see p. 98).

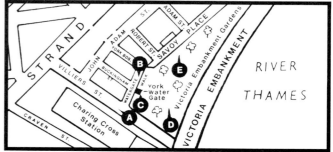

B   1779

C   1814

D   1870S

E   1890S

A *Villiers Street with hansom cabs pulling into the forecourt of Gatti's famous restaurant. The buildings on the right have changed but little; the left-hand side, however, was obliterated in 1990 by a monster office block.*

B *The York Water Gate with Westminster Bridge in the distance. The tower is part of the York Water Works and the steps, which still exist, lead up to Villiers Street.*

C *York Water Gate from the river with the Adelphi in the background. Of the two pedimented blocks at either end of the terrace, the one on the left still exists, the other can be seen in the Victorian photographs.*

D *Victoria Embankment Gardens just after they had been laid out in 1871.*

E *Hotel Cecil, opened in 1896, was the most magnificent hotel in Europe at the time. Replaced in 1930 by Shell-Mex House.*

A   C1875

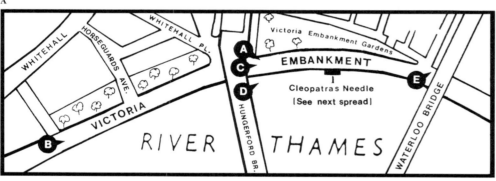

B   C1875

C   1911

The Embankment and Trams

BOTH THESE PHOTOGRAPHS (A and B) were taken between 1872 when the trees were planted, and 1878 when Cleopatra's Needle arrived. John Rennie's Waterloo Bridge of 1817 is seen in (A), while the bridge in (B) is Hungerford Railway Bridge opened in 1864.

Although electric trams arrived with the birth of the twentieth century, it was not until 1906 that they were allowed along the Embankment (C). In that year a tram tunnel had also been opened under Kingsway from Theobald's Road to a terminus at Aldwych. On 10 April 1908 an extension line was opened joining the Aldwych terminus to the Embankment via a tunnel with an exit by the side of Waterloo Bridge (E).

D C1895

E C1920

A *The Victoria Embankment just after it had opened.*

B *A photograph of about the same date taken from near Westminster Bridge.*

C *By 1911 trams had arrived.*

D *Dominating the skyline here are two great luxury hotels – the Cecil and the Savoy. A paddle steamer departs from Charing Cross Pier.*

E *A tram emerges from the Kingsway Tunnel by the side of Waterloo Bridge on its way to New Cross.*

A   1878

Cleopatra's Needle

AFTER A TURBULENT VOYAGE from Alexandria during which it was abandoned and thought to be lost, only to be picked up again, Cleopatra's Needle, encased in a cigar-like cylinder and towed by tugs, reached the Thames in January 1878. The site for the obelisk had not yet been decided upon and it was eight months before it was finally hoisted into position, at first horizontally (A) and then turned on a pivot to drop into its base. For a time the needle looked distinctly unstable balanced on its broken and irregular base (B) but these defects were soon hidden behind ornamental bronze castings. To these were added four panels giving a summary of the needle's history and acknowledging the people responsible for bringing it to London, including the names of six seamen who were drowned during its voyage.

The Mystery of the Sphinx

GEORGE VULLIAMY was commissioned to design a pair of Sphinxes to be mounted on the existing stone plinths on either side. As the engraving on the right shows, the original intention was to have the Sphinxes facing outwards (C) as indeed they are also shown in the photograph (D), where a full-size plaster model has been put in place to judge its effect. A close-up of the plaster model is shown in (E), painted to look like bronze. The Sphinxes were, however, erected facing inwards (F and G) as we see them today. They certainly look aesthetically more pleasing facing outwards, which gives support to the story that the contractors erected them the wrong way round and when the mistake was realized it was too late to rectify it.

B   C1879

C   1881

D   1880

F   C1882

E   1880

G   C1900

A *Cleopatra's Needle raised on its scaffolding*

B *Placed in position before the bronze casings were added.*

C *The Sphinxes in the position originally intended.*

D & E *A plaster Sphinx, painted to look like bronze, in its intended position.*

F & G *The Sphinxes as finally erected, the opposite way round.*

A   C1847

B   C1869

C   C1926

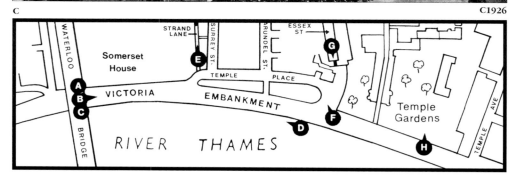

Somerset House to Blackfriars

WHEN SIR WILLIAM CHAMBERS built Somerset House between 1776 and 1796 he designed it with a riverside terrace on a basement storey rising out of the Thames itself (**A**). The splendid effect of its rusticated arches and water-gates was spoilt when the river was pushed back (**B**) and almost lost completely behind the raised roadway of the Embankment (**C** and **D**). Still surviving is the little Regency watch-house in Strand Lane with the so-called Roman Bath behind the railings (**E**), a charming view unaltered today except for the thoughtless imposition of unsympathetic street lighting. Another water-gate left high and dry by the Embankment is that once belonging to Essex House (**G**). Dating from the seventeenth century, it was badly damaged in the war but is still recognizable at the bottom of Essex Street where it leads to stairs which once went down to the river. The impressive office of the London School Board (**F**) erected in 1874 stood until 1931 when it was replaced by Electra House. To the right is a little gem of a building, happily still standing, built for Viscount Astor as his estate office in 1895 in Early Elizabethan style. Another convincing Tudor-style building which must have presented a pretty sight through the trees of Temple Gardens was Inner Temple Hall dating from only 1870 (**H**). It was destroyed in the blitz and its replacement built in 1955.

A, **B** & **C** *Three views of Somerset House showing how it was left high and dry by the building of the Embankment.*

D *Somerset House from the east. To its right is a fine Georgian house demolished in the 1880s.*

E *Strand Lane Watch-House.*

F *London School Board offices and Astor House.*

G *Essex House Water-gate.*

H *Inner Temple Hall glimpsed through the trees of Temple Gardens.*

E   1900S

D   C1880

F   C1896

G   1920S   H   C1880

A *City of London School just before Sion College was built on the open site on the left.*

B *De Keyser's Royal Hotel replaced by Unilever House in the 1930s.*

C *Blackfriars Underground Station on the District Line just after its opening in 1870.*

D *Blackfriars Bridge was a busy tram route. The railway bridge carried the London Chatham and Dover Railway and was called Alexandra Bridge.*

A

C1885

B

1919

Blackfriars

THE EXTRAORDINARY MOORISH BUILDING on the right (C), damaged in the war and recently demolished, was Blackfriars Underground Station, originally the eastern terminus of the District Line which was opened on 30 May 1870 and ran under the Embankment from Westminster Bridge. It was a terminus only until 3 July 1871 when the line was extended to Mansion House. The chimney to its right belonged to the City Flower Mill while to the left is the iron bridge carrying the London Chatham and Dover Railway to Ludgate Hill Station (see p.114). This line crossed the Thames on the Alexandra Bridge, the iron lattice-work structure seen by the side of Blackfriars Bridge in (D). Opened in 1864, it was the first railway bridge to cross the river within the City of London. It is now demolished but its cast-iron columns remain.

Blackfriars Bridge, here busy with trams linking the City with the huge South London network, was opened by Queen Victoria on 6 November 1869, the same day as she opened Holborn Viaduct.

The City of London School (A) remains unaffected by the road improvements hereabouts. It dates from 1882 and moved here from its original premises in Milk Street where it had been founded in the 1830s. The building is now used for offices.

On the site of old Bridewell Palace a huge, 400-room hotel (B) was built in the 1870s by Sir Polydore de Keyser who became the first Roman Catholic Lord Mayor since the Reformation. De Keyser's Royal Hotel closed soon after World War I, was taken over by Lever Brothers and rebuilt as Unilever House in 1931. On the right is the still-existing statue of Queen Victoria put up in 1893.

C   C1876

D   C1926

35668. London. Queen Victoria St C.N.

A   C1900

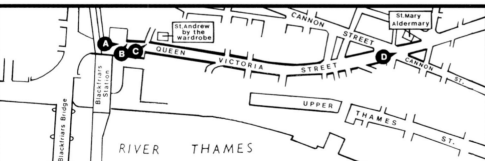

B   1880S

Queen Victoria Street

QUEEN VICTORIA STREET was authorized by Act of Parliament in 1863 but it was not completed until 1871, the delay caused by the construction of the District Railway beneath it. The importance of the new thoroughfare was appreciated by everyone for, as an extension of the Embankment, it linked the Houses of Parliament with the Bank of England, thus connecting the centres of legislation and commerce. Hundreds of old houses were destroyed in the creation of the new street but a few Georgian buildings managed to survive for a time (**B** and **C**). Those next door to the newly-built *Times* offices were soon replaced by the General Stores of Spiers & Pond, the railway caterers (**A**). One building which had anticipated the new street was the headquarters of the British & Foreign Bible Society whose foundation stone was laid as early as 1866. It stands next to the church of St Andrew-by-the-Wardrobe (**C**), once hidden from view, but whose south side was opened up by the building of the new street.

The church of St Mary Aldermary (**D**) had also been completely hemmed in originally. Opposite, the huge Gothic block on the corner of Cannon Street is almost all that survives from what was the greatest of all the improvements made to the City streets by the Victorians.

C 1870

A *Queen Victoria Street showing warehouses at the entrance to Upper Thames Street which were destroyed in the building of the recent road scheme.*

B *The newly-built* Times *Newspaper Offices.*

C *St Andrew-by-the-Wardrobe and the British & Foreign Bible Society unaltered today.*

D *The large Victorian building on the right still stands, as does the one behind the church of St Mary Aldermary.*

D 1890S

135

A   C1900

Cannon Street

Unlike Queen Victoria Street, Cannon Street is one of London's oldest thoroughfares and includes the City's most ancient feature, London Stone. This amorphous lump of limestone of unknown origin (but possibly a Roman milestone) was set in the wall of St Swithin's Church on the right of photo **(A)** where it is obscured by pedestrians. St Swithin's was demolished after bombing and the site is now occupied by the Bank of China who have reinstated the stone behind an iron grille. Just behind the lamp post is No. 103, one of the few surviving Victorian buildings in the street, dating from 1886. Opposite was Cannon Street Station Hotel **(c)** now gone in favour of a ghastly mess of offices and shops. **(B)** This important junction where five main thoroughfares converge still retains its Victorian shape although it has been entirely rebuilt. Prominent on the centre reservation was the statue of William IV erected in 1844 **(D)**. The increase in traffic and the danger of its enormous bulk (it was carved from solid granite) crashing through into the pedestrian subway being built beneath it

768 KING WILLIAM STREET.

B   1881

C 1880S

D 1880S

necessitated its removal. It was taken down in 1935 and re-erected near Greenwich Hospital, a fitting resting place for the Sailor King. King William Street (**E**) was created as the grand approach to the new London Bridge and was named after William IV who had opened it on 1 August 1831. Its continuation, ending at the Bank, can be seen in the centre of (**B**).

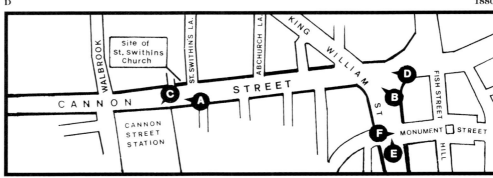

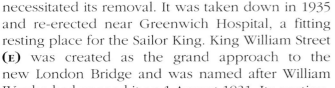

A Victorian Cannon Street with the church of St Swithin on the right. The Bank of China was built on its site in 1961.

B The busy junction where Cannon Street joins King William Street in 1881.

C The terminus hotel of Cannon Street Station designed by E.M. Barry in the 1860s.

D The granite statue of William IV erected in 1844 and removed to Greenwich in 1935.

E The southern end of King William Street named after William IV to commemorate his opening of London Bridge in 1831.

F The Monument seen from King William Street.

E 1890S

F C1883

137

A

1926

Around the Monument

T HE CLAMOUR AND BUSTLE of Billingsgate, typified in the photo above, is now only a nostalgic memory (A). St Magnus and the Monument can still be seen from here and the streets are the same but gone are the fish porters with crates on their heads and the wet cobbles no longer bring a smell of the seaside to the heart of London. For in 1982 the fish market was moved out to the Isle of Dogs and Billingsgate will never be the same again.

Fish Street Hill was originally the only thoroughfare leading to Old London Bridge. Until the 1750s the bridge had houses built upon it which can be seen just beyond the projecting clock of St Magnus the Martyr in the eighteenth-century engraving (c). When the church was built, the houses on the bridge came right up to its walls on either side. Once the houses were removed, the church stood out over the pavement forcing pedestrians into the road. The solution was to cut an opening through the tower, a necessity which Wren had anticipated by building his tower with archways lightly filled in. With the filling removed, the tower now had arches through which pedestrians could walk in safety (D). When Old London Bridge was demolished and New London Bridge was built 180 feet (54 metres) up river, Fish Street Hill lost its importance. All the original houses on the western side were demolished when the approach road to the new bridge was cut through their backyards. They were rebuilt as a unified terrace (B) which included the Weigh House Chapel, the pedimented building on the right, which was demolished in 1883 to make way for Monument Underground Station. The eastern side, including the Monument, was virtually unchanged by the removal of the bridge. By the side of St Magnus a hotel and office block was erected and when this was removed in 1921 a delightful view of the river and New London Bridge was revealed (E). This lasted only until the present Adelaide House rose up to ruin the view in 1924.

B

C1882

C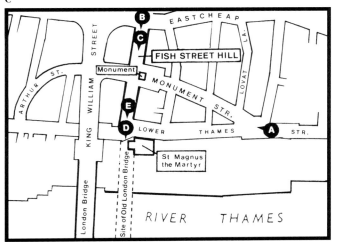

D

A *Billingsgate Market with St Magnus and the Monument.*

B *Fish Street Hill before Monument Station arrived.*

C *Fish Street Hill in the early eighteenth century showing houses on Old London Bridge.*

D *St Magnus the Martyr with a footpath through its tower on to the bridge after the removal of the houses.*

E *The view across the river before Adelaide House was built.*

C1740

1814

E   C1923

30688. LONDON BRIDGE. C.N.

A

C   C1900

London Bridge

ALL THAT IS RECOGNIZABLE in this Victorian photograph (A) is Fishmongers' Hall on the left. The scene began to change in 1920 when the block opposite Fishmongers' Hall, occupied by the Pearl Life Assurance Company, was demolished (B). Four years later, the ten-storey Adelaide House had arisen on the site and Londoners, gazing on their first skyscraper, wondered what had happened to the Monument and St Magnus the Martyr. For the first time since the Great Fire they no longer dominated the skyline and Adelaide House still hides them from view. The London Bridge seen above, which is now basking in the Arizona sun having been transported to America, stone by stone, in 1968, is not quite as we remember it. In 1902 it was widened and the solid parapet removed. The extra 5ft 9in (1.75 metres) on either side was supported on granite brackets and the new footpaths were lined with open balustrades as can be seen in the later photograph (B). These new additions were the first stones to arrive in America, allowed in duty free, officially certified by the US Customs as 'a large antique' although they were a mere sixty years old. The view from Fishmongers' Hall (C) shows the new Tower Bridge in the distance. Before it was built the view down river (E) was very different.

B   1920

A & B *London Bridge in about 1900 and some twenty years later.*

C *The view down river soon after Tower Bridge was built.*

D *Traffic approaching London Bridge from Borough High Street.*

E *The river before Tower Bridge. On the left is the Customs House.*

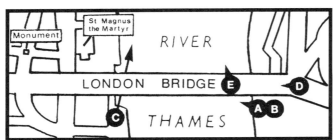

C1900   **D**   C1890

E   C1890

A   C1838

B   C1851

Borough High Street 1

IN 1831 THE BUILDING of New London Bridge some 180 feet (54 metres) to the west of the old changed the original direction of Borough High Street and it was altered and widened to form a new approach. Among the improvements was the creation of a large open space with gardens surrounding the newly-built North Wing of St Thomas's Hospital which can be seen on the left of (**A**). It was to serve as an attractive approach to London Bridge Station when the railway arrived. This was London's first railway, the London to Greenwich, which was opened in 1836. Originally there was no station here worthy of the name but a mere starting yard devoid of buildings. Soon other branch lines were constructed to terminate at this spot and by 1851, when the engraving (**B**) was published, a permanent station had been built, parts of which can be identified in the Victorian photograph (**C**). The block on the right is the station hotel dating from 1861 which was demolished after bomb damage during the war. So far the railway had caused only minor disruptions to the High Street but in 1864 a traumatic change took place from which it has never recovered. This was the building of the ugly girder bridge to carry the West End extension to Charing Cross. To avoid Southwark Cathedral it had to swerve south-west and in doing so it cut across a small corner of the grounds of St Thomas's Hospital. Although only one-sixth of an acre was needed, the hospital governors forced the railway company to buy the entire property and they rebuilt the hospital on the Albert Embankment. A fragment of the old hospital is now a post office.

C   C1900

As early as 1840 it was proposed to form a new thoroughfare linking the Borough with the West End to ease the congestion caused by the railway termini at London Bridge Station but it was not until 1857 that the plan was carried out. The result was the creation of Southwark Street, the first part of which was opened in 1862 just two years before the railway viaduct was thrown across it (**D**).

For one of the most historic thoroughfares in London, Borough High Street (**E**) was, and still is, surprisingly featureless. Its interest lies hidden behind its bland façades.

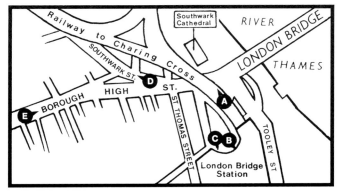

D   1890S

A *The view of Southwark Cathedral from the* approach road to London's first railway. B & C *London Bridge Station 50 years apart.* D *Southwark Street with the Charing Cross railway* extension. E *Borough High Street.*

E   1890S

143

A   1896

Borough High Street 2

EVER SINCE THE EARLIEST TIMES Borough High Street has been the gateway to London from the south along which all traffic had to pass on its way to London Bridge. Not surprising, then, that it was liberally supplied with taverns to refresh the weary traveller and great inns which offered accommodation and served as depots for the carrier waggons and passenger coaches plying to and from the south-east of England. Of these dozens of inns ('Great rambling, queer old places' Dickens called them) only one exists today – The George (A) though it is but a shadow of its former self. It was built in 1676 after its predecessor had been destroyed by fire. Originally, with its extensive stabling, it covered acres of ground but in 1889 it was bought by a railway company which pulled down most of it. The fragment which still survives was given to the National Trust and remains as London's only example of a galleried coaching inn. On the other side of the High Street is another seventeenth-century survivor, in Calvert's Buildings (B). The timber-framed house with its typical overhang may well have been an inn originally.

B   1926

A *The George. Through the arch at the back can be seen the stable-yards which were later built over.*

B *The seventeenth-century house in Calvert's Buildings, hardly changed today.*

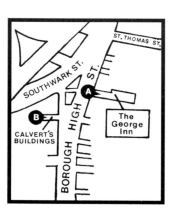

KENSINGTON AND CHELSEA

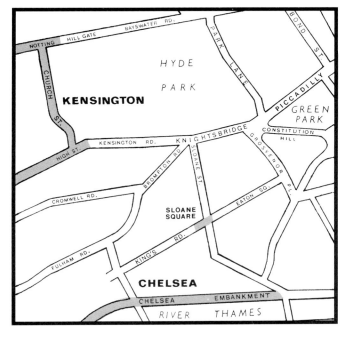

KENSINGTON AND CHELSEA were joined together, in spite of protests, with the reorganization of the Metropolitan Boroughs in 1964. Until then they were very separate entities whose original village centres were a mile and a half apart.

Notting Hill was on the main Uxbridge Road where the toll-gate stood and from which a country lane wound down the hill to the village of Kensington. It still does today, but the old village is now all traffic and commercial bustle, with the great art deco block of Barker's dominating the scene. Big as it is, it fails to overwhelm the mid-Victorian church of St Mary Abbots, for its famous spire is the tallest in London.

It was due to the express wish of Queen Victoria, who was born in Kensington Palace, that the borough became 'Royal'. This only served to confirm the already aristocratic feel of the place, for the rich merchants and upper middle classes had been building their great houses here to get away from the noise of the crowded City since the beginning of the nineteenth century. High-class shops were established to serve the families of the rich, and with the arrival of the Underground, and later the huge American-style department stores, Kensington High Street became an extension of the West End.

Chelsea's story is a little different. Here the village nucleus around the old parish church has not been commercialized. The traffic-laden Embankment apart, the area can still feel quiet and restful and Cheyne Walk, with its trees and unspoilt eighteenth-century houses, has a village charm all its own. This is the real essence of Chelsea, a far cry from the brash noise and bustle of Sloane Square and the King's Road where the Swinging Sixties were born.

RIGHT *An 1860s photograph of St Mary Abbots, Kensington.*

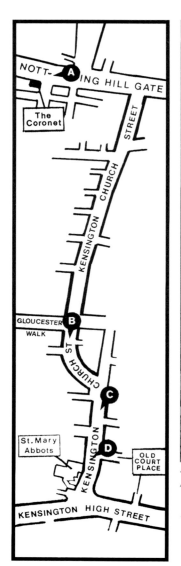

C1900

A The Coronet Notting Hill Gate with three more humble survivors on the left.

B An extra horse helps the omnibus up the hill of Kensington Church Street.

C A block of flats called York House was built in 1904 on the vacant site opposite these Victorian buildings.

D Just north of St Mary Abbots, these houses were built around 1760 and still survive.

B

C1906

C   C1903

Notting Hill Gate to Kensington

THE NAME RECALLS the old turnpike toll-gate which stood here until 1864. It has always been a busy traffic route and as early as the 1920s its congestion was causing such concern that in 1937 the LCC obtained permission to widen the street. The war intervened and it was not until 1957 that work began. The result was an almost complete transformation of Victorian Notting Hill Gate, although some early buildings can still be identified adjacent to the Coronet Theatre (A). This was opened with a production of *The Geisha* on 28 November 1898, when it was described as 'a theatre of which the whole County of London may be proud'. It was adapted as a cinema as early as 1916. The magnificent hanging lamps on the right belong to the Coach & Horses pub.

Kensington Church Street remained a country lane, with a few eighteenth-century houses at either end, until well into Victoria's reign. Half-way down, the first houses to be built were those on the corner of Gloucester Walk (B). Dating from 1845, they still stand today. Round the bend, the whole of the east side has been rebuilt, but all the buildings opposite (C) have remained unchanged since they were erected in 1882. Even more striking survivals are these houses (D) which were built sometime before 1760. The ground floors are now shops but 'Simpson & Annett' still retains its original door and railings. The photo was taken from Old Court Place two years before this side was widened in 1913.

D   1911

A   C1865

B   C1865

Kensington Village

THE APPROACH TO KENSINGTON was once hardly wider than a country lane and so unfamiliar to us today that it is difficult to visualize the viewpoints in the early photographs (A and B). But by identifying the archway in (A) with the same archway which appears in (D) and (F) all is made clear. We are, in fact, looking west along Kensington High Street before all the buildings on the left were demolished leaving the open space seen in (F) later to be the site of Barker's department store. The archway, which still exists, leading today to Kensington Church Court, was originally the entrance to the Crown Inn stable-yard but was made residential in 1722. Surprisingly, fragments which escaped the road widening do still survive from the ancient highway and they all appear in the photograph dated 1909 (C). The building on the left with the bay windows, No. 17, was built about 1695 and was a pub called the Green Man in its early days. Next door, Nos. 19 and 21 were also built in the 1690s and Nos. 23 and 25 date from 1782. Though there have been some alterations, especially to the ground floor shop-fronts, none of these properties has been rebuilt. The old country village of Kensington enjoyed a sudden prosperity when, in 1690, William and Mary arrived at Nottingham House, later to become Kensington Palace. It was then that the medieval parish church of St Mary's was rebuilt except for the tower (D) which was added in 1770. The old church was declared unsafe at the time this photograph (E) was taken and in 1869 it was demolished (F). On the left is the familiar archway and on the right of both photographs is The Civit Cat (see next page).

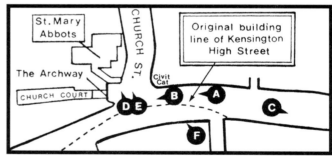

A & B *These mid-nineteenth-century photographs show how extraordinarily narrow the High Street was opposite the church. All these buildings were demolished in 1869 when the road was widened.*

C *Nos. 17–25 (odd) Kensington High Street. Built in 1692 and 1782, they still stand today.*

D *St Mary Abbots Church in the middle of the eighteenth century.*

E *The same view just over one hundred years later.*

F *St Mary Abbots being demolished in 1869. The cleared foreground became the site of Barker's department store.*

C   1909

D   **C1750**

E   **C1860**

F   **1869**

A   C1896

B   C1904

Kensington High Street

WITH THE WIDENING of the thoroughfare and the opening of the underground railway, the High Street began to flourish and new businesses were created to attract a high-class clientele away from the West End. It heralded the age of the great department store. The pretty neo-Jacobean Vestry Hall (A) was built in 1852 but soon proved too small for municipal affairs and a new Town Hall was built next to it in 1880. The old Vestry Hall became the public library and still stands though it is now a bank. The Town Hall was less fortunate: it was wantonly damaged by a demolition gang one weekend in 1982 before efforts to protect it as a listed building could be implemented. It was finally demolished two years later.

Just below the hanging lamp in (A) is the pub on the corner of Church Street called The Civit Cat. By 1904 it had been rebuilt as we see it today (B and C) with its hanging sign topped by a delightful model of a civit cat. It became a bank in 1919 but the pub signs still hang outside. The column erected in memory of Queen Victoria in 1904, nicknamed 'The Chocolate Stick' (C) was moved to Warwick Gardens in 1934. Kensington Station (E) was opened on 1 October 1868 and here announces 'City & Bank 4d. Either Way'.

C   Kensington, High Street.   C1907

D   C1905

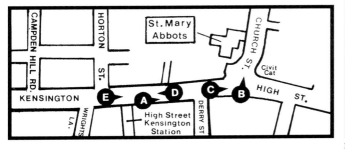

E   1905

A   *All that survives in this photograph is the mid-Victorian Vestry Hall.*

B   *The still-existing sign of The Civit Cat can be seen just below the chimney-pots.*

C   *To the right of 'The Chocolate Stick' memorial is Barker's, rebuilt as we see it now in 1933.*

D   *Looking west with Pontings on the left.*

E   *The Town Hall Tavern, built in 1868, was swallowed up by Derry & Toms in 1912.*

A   1811

B   1906

C   C1890

The Old High Street

THE NORTH SIDE OF THE HIGH STREET was one long ribbon development of terrace houses in the early nineteenth century **(A)**. They did not become shops until 1905 when their front gardens were removed **(B)**. At the same time Hornton Court was built, a block of flats which still exists and which can be seen on the right of **(B)**. The terrace was demolished in 1931.

A similar terrace was built on the opposite side of the road between 1818 and 1821. It was called Allen Terrace after its builder and the corner block still survives. The shops were added in 1877 **(E)**. Adjacent to this terrace was a more humble row built at the same time **(C)** that has now completely disappeared. A remarkable survival is this block **(D)** built in 1882. It is on the corner of Adam & Eve Mews, a name which perpetuates the memory of an inn dating back to the seventeenth century when Kensington ended here and there were no more houses until Hammersmith.

D

C1900

E

C1905

Sloane Square

By the 1890s most of the Georgian houses surrounding the village green which became Sloane Square were replaced by Victorian blocks, many of which still remain (**D** and **E**). The church in (**D**) is Holy Trinity, consecrated in 1890, and greatly admired by Sir John Betjeman who called it 'the cathedral of the Arts and Crafts'.

Sloane Square Underground Station, behind the tree on the left of (**B**), was opened on Christmas Eve 1868 and it was not until March 1940 that it was modernized with the installation of escalators, finally ending the complaints from generations of passengers tramping up and down fifty-one stairs. Eight months later a bomb dropped right on the station, demolishing it and the new escalators. The same bomb also damaged the Royal Court Theatre, just to the left of the tree. It had been opened in 1888 but it was not until renovation after the Second World War that it made its name in theatrical history with the production of avant-garde plays.

Since 1936 Peter Jones has dominated the west end of the square. The earlier store, however, fronted on King's Road (**A**) with a large pub, The Star & Garter, on the Sloane Square corner (**C**). This pub was bought by Peter Jones in 1911 and proved to be such a financial asset that it was allowed to remain in operation as a public house until the rebuilding in the 1930s.

A

C1905

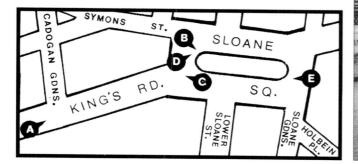

B

1895

C1897

1900S

E

1900S

A The old Peter Jones building from the King's Road, now completely rebuilt. The block on the left, built in 1887, still survives.

B The Georgian houses and shops on the south side of Sloane Square were replaced in 1906 by the large white stone block which stands today.

C The Star & Garter pub on the corner of King's Road. Behind it is the old Peter Jones building.

D Little has changed in this view today. The central block was built between 1895 and 1898 and the church at the end of Sloane Street is Holy Trinity.

E Though Peter Jones was separated from the square by other buildings, its tower still dominated the view.

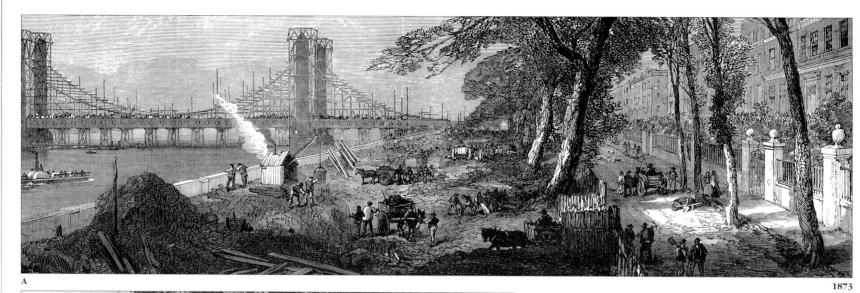

A

1873

Chelsea Embankment

T HE CONSTRUCTION OF THE EMBANKMENT in the 1870s **(A)** totally changed the appearance of Chelsea's riverside, destroying the picturesque wharves and boathouses beloved of Victorian artists. Like the Victoria Embankment, it was designed by Bazalgette as an extension to his scheme for the drainage of the metropolis. But it had no effect on the terraces of Georgian houses **(B)** which remained, and still remain, aloof from all the bustle of the Embankment. Things were to change radically, however, when the road reached Chelsea Old Church.

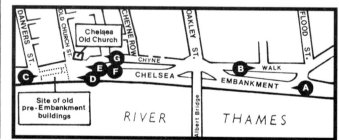

B

C1875

A *The Embankment being built, with Albert Bridge also under construction.*

B *Cheyne Walk just after the Embankment had been built. At the road junction at the end, the great Queen Anne-style mansions of Norman Shaw and others would appear in the next few years.*

C *The road through Arch House called Lombard Street with Danvers Street on the left.*

C

C1870

D *Chelsea Old Church after a drawing by Chatelain.*

E *The monument to Sir Hans Sloane, on the corner of the churchyard, was erected in 1763, ten years after his death.*

F *Part of this terrace still remains.*

G *Cheyne Hospital was built on the site of the house where Holman Hunt painted 'The Light of the World'.*

D   **1750**

Chelsea Old Church

FOR CENTURIES THE RIVERSIDE THOROUGHFARE ended abruptly just west of the church where a building called the Arch House straddled the road (**D**). Through the arch was a clutter of old houses (**C**) going down to the water's edge which were all swept away when the Embankment arrived. Apart from the modifications to the tower, Chelsea Old Church looks much the same in all these illustrations and today; in spite of being damaged in the Second World War, its careful restoration gives the impression that it has never changed. Remarkably, the houses just to the right of the church, built in the 1680s, have survived until now: the large red-brick block (**G**) was built in 1888 as the Cheyne Hospital for Sick & Incurable Children.

E   **1829**

F   **C1870**

G   **1893**

PICTURE SOURCES

PHOTOGRAPHS

The majority of photographs in this book are from my own collection and a great many of them are from original glass negatives which, about thirty years ago, I was fortunate enough to acquire from York & Son, a firm of photographers that produced lantern slides, stereograms and postcards from the 1870s to the 1920s. These photographs are not acknowledged here.

The following photographs come from other sources:

National Monuments Record, 25D, 26D, 29C, 36B, 38D, 39G, 40A and B, 41D and G, 43D and E, 58A, 68C, 69G, 71E, 72B, 75D, 76A, 99E, 100A and D, 101G, 103C and E, 104B, 106B, 107E and F, 109J, 110B, 111G, 113B, 132B, 135C, 145, 148A and B, 149E and F, 151E, 156B and C, 157F and G.
Westminster Library, 68A, 105C.
Kensington Library, 10A and B, 147D, 150B, 153E.
Chelsea Library, 155E.
Society of Antiquaries, 71G and H.

PRINTS AND DRAWINGS

All the prints and drawings are from my own collection. The names of artists and engravers are given when they are known and, as many of the prints were originally published as book illustrations, every effort has been made to identify the books in which they first appeared, a task made easy thanks to Bernard Adams's indispensable catalogue *London Illustrated* (1983).

The following abbreviations are used:

Ackermann	Aquatint from *Ackermann's Repository of Arts* (1809–29)
ILN	Wood engraving from *The Illustrated London News*
LTS	London Topographical Society
Malton	Aquatint from Thomas Malton's *A Picturesque Tour Through the Cities of London & Westminster* (1792)
Shepherd	Engraving after Thomas Hosmer Shepherd from *Metropolitan Improvements or London in the Nineteenth Century* (1827–30)
Shotter Boys	Lithograph from *Original Views of London as it is* by Thomas Shotter Boys (1842)
Tallis	From Tallis's *London Street Views* (1838–40)

14 (A) Aquatint by and after Dagaty, 1797. (B) Aquatint by Hall after Dayes from Hunter's *History of London* (1811). (C) Shotter Boys.
15 (D) Anon. lithograph.
16 (A) Engraving by A. Bairns after Schrubellee (*sic*).
17 (C) Engraving from Cassell's *Old & New London*.
18 (B) Etching by J. Malcolm from his *Anecdotes of the Manners & Customs of London* (1808).
20 (A) Tallis. (D) Engraving from Partington's *National History & Views of London* (1835).
21 (E) Engraving by and after S. Rawle from *European Magazine* 1804. (F) Shepherd. (G) Shotter Boys. (I) Tallis.
22 (C) Drawing by J. P. Emslie, dated July 29, 1885.
24 (B) Lithograph by and after Ch. Riviere from *Vues de Londres*, Paris (ND).
26 (A) Shepherd.
28 (A) Drawing by J. P. Emslie.
29 (D) ILN, October 18, 1845.
30 (A) Tallis. (B) Engraving by F. J. Havell after William and Frederick Havell.

31 (D) Malton. (E) Anon. engraving. (F) Engraving by Rooker after P. Sandby.
32 (A) Engraving by and after Charles John Smith from his *Historical & Literary Curiosities* (1836). (B) Ackermann. (C) Engraving by Busby after Wichelo from *Beauties of England & Wales* (1801–18). (D) Shepherd. (E) Engraving from *Mighty London* (1851–2).
34 (A) Ackermann.
37 (E) Ackermann.
41 (C) Ackermann.
47 (E) ILN, September 28, 1867.
50 (A) Lithograph made from a photograph. (C) Aquatint drawn and etched by J. Buckler, engraved by F. C. Lewis, 1804.
53 (C) Malton.
55 (D) Engraving by J. Le Keux after R. W. Billings, from Godwin's *Churches of London* (1839). (F) Engraving by W. H. Toms after R. West from West and Toms's *Ancient Churches* (1736–9).
56 (A) Engraving by George Cooke after C. Stanfield, from Cooke's *Views in London & its Vicinity* (1826–34).
60 (B) Tallis.
61 (D) Aquatint by S. Alken after W. C. Lochner. (E) Shepherd.
62 (A) Engraving by and after Thomas Highman.
63 (C) Aquatint by and after Thomas Malton (Single plate, not from *Picturesque Tour*).
64 (A) Malton. (B) Shepherd.
68 (B) *Pictorial Times*, April 10, 1847.
69 (E and F) Engraving by and after J. T. Smith, from his *Antiquities of Westminster* (1807).
70 (A) Aquatint by and after Robert Havell & Son. (B) Anon. mezzotint. (C) Lithograph by C. Burton after Samuel Russell.
74 (A) Drawing by Capon. Society of Antiquaries. Reproduced in *Views of Westminster* published by LTS (1923–4).
75 (E) Shepherd.
76 (C) ILN, September 23, 1854.
79 (D) ILN, January 3, 1846.
82 (A) Engraving by J. B. Allen after G. Hawkins. (B) Engraving by and after J. Maurer. (C) Shepherd. (D) Shotter Boys.
84 (A) Shepherd. (C) Ackermann.
85 (E) Ackermann. (F) No. 3 of Lacey's *Select Views of London* (*c.*1827).
86 (B) Shepherd.
87 (E) Shepherd.

88 (A) Engraving by Thomas Higham after G. Moore. (B) Ackermann. (C) Shotter Boys.
89 (F) Aquatint by R. Reeve after C. Wild, from Payne's *Royal Residences* (1819).
90 (A) Tallis. (C) ILN, April 27, 1844.
92 (A) Tallis.
94 (A, B and C) Malton.
95 (D) Drawing by J. P. Emslie, from *Illustrated Topographical Record of London*, published by ILN, 1899.
98 (B and C) Malton.
101 (F) Tallis.
102 (B) Drawing by F. L. Emanuel, reproduced as a supplement to *Architectural Review* (June 1900).
106 (A) Shotter Boys.
108 (A) Anon. engraving. (B) Engraving by Warren after Schnebbelie from Hughson's *Description of London* (1811). (C) Tallis.
109 (G) Anon. engraving from Colnaghi's *Select Views* (1795–1800). (H) Engraving by George Cooke after D. Roberts, from Cooke's *Views in London & its Vicinity* (1826–34).
111 (D) Anon. aquatint.
114 (A) Ackermann.
116 (A) Shotter Boys. (C) Malton. (D) Lithograph from *Horner's View of London* (1823).
117 (G) Lithograph from *Horner's View of London* (1823).
124 (B) Engraving from *The Modern Universal British Traveller* (1779).
125 (C) Anon. aquatint.
128 (C) *Graphic* (July 2, 1881).
130 (A) Engraving from Payne's *Illustrated London* (*c.*1847).
131 (G) Etching by Edgar A. Holloway.
139 (C) Engraving by T. F. Leizel. (D) Engraving by W. Wise after G. Shepherd, from *Architectura Ecclesiastica Londini* (1820). (E) Drawing by Philip Norman, publication No. 70, LTS (1936).
142 (A) Engraving by Shury after G. J. Shepherd. (B) Engraving from Tallis's *Illustrated London* (*c.* 1851).
149 (D) Anon. engraving published by Laurie & Whittle (*c.* 1750).
152 (A) From Salway's *Kensington Turnpike Trust Plans*, LTS (1899–1903).
156 (A) ILN, June 14, 1873.
158 (D) Engraving by I. Roberts after Chatelain from Chatelain's *Fifty Original Views* (1750). (E) Shepherd.

INDEX